Gift
of Peace

Other Books in the
Zonderkidz Biography Series:

Gift of Peace

the

Jimmy Carter Story

Elizabeth Raum

ZONDERVAN.com/
AUTHORTRACKER
follow your favorite authors

ZONDERKIDZ

Gift of Peace: The Jimmy Carter Story
Copyright © 2011 by Elizabeth Raum

This title is also available as a Zondervan ebook.
Visit www.zondervan.com/ebooks

Requests for information should be addressed to:

Zonderkidz, *Grand Rapids, Michigan* 49530

Library of Congress Cataloging-in-Publication Data

Raum, Elizabeth.
    Gift of peace : the Jimmy Carter story / Elizabeth Raum.
       p. cm. — (Zonderkidz biography series)
    ISBN 978-0-310-72756-9 (softcover)
    1. Carter, Jimmy, 1924- — Juvenile literature. 2. Presidents—United States—Biography—
Juvenile literature. I. Title.
E873.R38 2011
973.926092—dc23
  [B]   2011024821

Art direction: Ben Fetterley
Cover design: Kris Nelson
Interior design and composition: Greg Johnson/Textbook Perfect

Printed in the United States of America

---

11 12 13 14 15 16 /DCI/ 21 20 19 18 17 16 15 14 13 12 11 10 9 8 7 6 5 4 3 2 1

Table of Contents

Table of Contents

Chapter 1

Helping Out

In 1976, Jimmy Carter ran for president of the United States, and America went nuts—peanuts, that is. Few people outside of the South recognized his name. Who was Jimmy Carter? He needed a way to introduce himself to the voters, and peanuts paved the way. Jimmy ran his family's peanut business. He grew up on a farm and sold bagfuls on the streets of Georgia as a child. Jimmy chose a big smiling peanut as his **campaign** logo. He and his family gave away buttons and bags of roasted nuts that read, "Jimmy Carter For President." Men wore gold peanut pins and women wore peanut necklaces. Jimmy flew from state to state in an

Jimmy, whose full name is James Earl Carter Jr., was born at the Wise Hospital in Plains, Georgia, on October 1, 1924. Jimmy was the first United States president to be born in a hospital. Until the 1920s, most women gave birth at home. Jimmy's mother, a nurse, believed that hospital births were safer for mother and baby than home births.

Gift of Peace

Supporters in Evanston, Illinois, welcomed Jimmy to their town by building a thirteen-foot peanut with a grin as big as Jimmy Carter's. Located in Plains, Georgia, it may not be the biggest peanut sculpture in the world, but it's the happiest.

airplane called Peanut One, and his supporters called themselves the Peanut Brigade. It was nutty.

Of course, there was much more to Jimmy Carter than farming. He fought for civil rights, served in the navy, and had been elected Georgia's governor. He was a husband, a dad, and an active member of his church. It was Jimmy Carter's honesty and willingness to help others that convinced voters to elect him president of the United States.

Today, thirty years after leaving the White House, he continues to work hard and help others throughout the nation and around the world.

"First useful act"

Jimmy Carter learned to help others at a young age from the influence of his parents. His mother, Lillian Gordy Carter, studied nursing at the Wise Hospital in Plains, Georgia. That's where she met Jimmy's dad, James Earl Carter Sr., a local businessman. Jimmy's parents, who everyone called Miss Lillian and Mr. Earl, provided him and his sisters with a safe and loving home, first in Plains, a town of about six hundred people, and then in the smaller community of Archery, Georgia.

On the day that Jimmy's dad, Mr. Earl, took Jimmy, Gloria, and Miss Lillian to see their new home in Archery, he forgot the key. It was two and a half miles back to Plains, so Mr. Earl tried to pry open a window. It was stuck, and he could only open it a crack. The narrow opening was far too small for a big man like Mr. Earl, so he slid Jimmy inside. Jimmy ran to the front door and

Jimmy was four years old, and his sister Gloria was two, when the Carters moved to a farm in Archery, Georgia.

unlocked it. Jimmy later called it his "first useful act." Nothing pleased Jimmy more than being helpful.

At home in Archery

The Carters's house in Archery was square and painted white. Cars passing by the highway kicked up so much dust that the house took on the brownish-red color of the dirt. The house had no running water or bathrooms inside. Jimmy drew water from the well in the yard and hauled it to the house for cooking, laundry, and washing up. Extra buckets of water were stored on the back porch. The family used a "two-holer," an outhouse (or privy) with two holes for toilets. The larger one was for adults, and a smaller one was reserved for children—it kept them from falling in! The Carters took recycling seriously long before everyone understood its importance. Instead of toilet paper, they used old newspapers or pages torn from a Sears Roebuck catalog.

Although Jimmy's home wasn't big and fancy, his family was better off than many others. During the 1930s, when Jimmy was a boy, the **Great Depression** left many people jobless, homeless, and hungry. Farms failed, factories closed, and people lost their homes to the bank. Children as young as six or seven went to work, trying to earn a few pennies for food.

The Carter house sat beside a main highway. Often, single men traveled past on their way west looking for jobs. Occasionally, entire families took to the roads seeking a better life. Homeless travelers like these were called tramps. Many stopped at the Carter home hoping to find work or something to eat. If Jimmy's mother, Miss Lillian, was home, she never turned anyone away. She always gave them some food to help them on their way.

One day Miss Lillian was talking to a neighbor. "I'm thankful that they never come in my yard," the neighbor said.

The next time a tramp knocked on Miss Lillian's door, she asked why he stopped at her house and not others.

"The post on your mailbox is marked to say that you don't turn people away or mistreat us," he said. He explained that tramps used a set of rough symbols to help them find people who would help them out.

Courtesy of the Jimmy Carter National Historic Site

The house in Archery had two porches, a wide one in front facing the road, and a smaller one in back.

Jimmy and his sisters checked the mailbox. They discovered a series of nearly invisible scratches on the post. When Jimmy turned to his mother, she told him not to change those marks. He learned from his mother's example that it's important to help others, even those you don't know and may never see again.

As he grew older, Jimmy put these lessons to work. No matter where he was or what office he held, Jimmy Carter never forgot the importance of helping others.

Chapter 2

Jimmy's Early Life

Mr. Earl loved to play tennis. Soon after moving to Archery, he built a tennis court near the house. He taught Jimmy to play tennis too. But no matter how hard he tried, Jimmy could never beat his dad! Mr. Earl also dug a small swimming pool behind the house. It was a great place to swim, except for one *big* problem. Sometimes, poisonous snakes slithered from the nearby swamps into the pool. The children always checked the pool carefully before diving into the water.

Jimmy spent most of his time outdoors. He didn't have much in common with his younger sisters. Gloria was two years younger than Jimmy. Ruth, born after the family moved to Archery, was three years younger. Neither of them worked in the barn or fields like Jimmy did. They spent their time sewing, cooking, or playing with dolls. The entire family came together for meals

In this elementary
school photo,
Jimmy shows his
world-famous smile.

Courtesy of the Jimmy Carter Library

and for church on Sunday. Sometimes, in the winter, the children played board games at the dining room table before bed. From time to time, their parents took them to Americus, fourteen miles away, to see a movie. Jimmy's only brother, Billy, wasn't born until Jimmy was twelve.

During the summers, the Carters spent their evenings on the front porch sitting on rocking chairs or the porch swing. On winter evenings, they lit the fireplace in the living room. **Kerosene** lamps provided light as they gathered around a large battery-powered radio and listened to the big band music of Glenn Miller or to comedy programs like *Amos 'n Andy* or *Fibber McGee and*

Molly. Sometimes they heard sports announcers describing faraway baseball games or boxing matches.

During the summers, daytime was work time. Jimmy spent long hours helping his father. Mr. Earl always called Jimmy *Hot* or *Hot Shot.* "Hot, would you like to pick cotton this afternoon?" Mr. Earl would ask. Hot always said yes. He wanted to live up to his father's high expectations. "My father was my hero," Jimmy later wrote. "I watched his every move with admiration."

Jimmy got up at 4:00 a.m. when the big farm bell called workers to the fields. He watched farmhands gather supplies by lantern light, hitch the mules to the wagons, and drive to the fields as the sun came up. As soon as he was big enough to carry a bucket, Jimmy's father put him to work hauling water to the field workers. He carried an empty bucket in each hand to the spring, which was usually located at the bottom of a steep hill in a boggy area. Water sloshed out of the heavy buckets as Jimmy carried them back to the workers. They gulped down the water and sent Jimmy back for more.

Mr. Earl encouraged Jimmy to earn money as a businessman. Jimmy was only five years old when his dad sent him to Plains to sell peanuts on a street corner. The season lasted about two months, starting in mid-July. At first, Jimmy sold bags of peanuts that his father prepared. As he got older, he helped prepare the peanuts. Peanut seeds grow into green, oval-shaped bushes that send tiny vines into the ground. Most vines produce about fifty nuts. When the peanuts were ripe, Jimmy pulled the vines. He washed and soaked the peanuts in salt water overnight, and then early the next morning, he boiled the peanuts for thirty minutes and put them into paper sacks before going to town to sell nuts.

Jimmy had about ten regular customers. He also sold nuts to shoppers visiting Plains. Sometimes the men playing cards and swapping stories at the gas stations bought a bag or two. On good days, Jimmy sold his entire supply by noon and returned home with a dollar's worth of change. Other days, the card players teased Jimmy and tried to get him to do chores for them. Selling the peanuts wasn't easy, but as Jimmy later admitted, it was good training. When he became governor of Georgia, he proudly declared, "I have always attempted to conduct my business in an honest and efficient manner."

School

Jimmy began first grade in Plains just before he turned six. On the farm and with his friends, Jimmy felt self-confident. But when he left home to attend school in Plains, he became shy and timid. Jimmy was small for his age, and he wasn't used to competing against other white boys. He knew a few of the children from church, but there were many he didn't know. He gathered his courage, walked up to those he didn't know, put out his hand, and said, "Hi, I'm Jimmy Carter."

The school day began with a chapel service, prayer, and the singing of a patriotic song. Morning classes followed and then lunch. Jimmy's father arranged for Jimmy (and later Gloria, as well) to eat at his Aunt Ethel and Uncle Willard's house near the school. Sometimes

Aunt Ethel was slow in preparing the meal, which bothered Jimmy. He didn't want to miss playing baseball or other sports with the boys on the playground during recess. Jimmy waited patiently, but he was always eager to get back to school.

Jimmy could read and write before he began school. He loved reading. In third grade, he won a contest for reading the most books. As a reward, he ate dinner with his teacher, Miss Tot. Jimmy wore his best clothes for the big event. His excitement gave way to shock when Miss Tot served sauerkraut, a pickled cabbage dish. Jimmy had never eaten sauerkraut before. He thought it looked and tasted like a big mistake. Nevertheless, he ate it all. The other part of the reward pleased him more. Miss Tot gave him a framed print of a famous painting by Thomas Gainsborough. Jimmy hung it in his room. The picture more than made up for his struggle with the sauerkraut.

All the teachers encouraged their students to read. Miss Julia Coleman, the school superintendent, insisted on it. Miss Julia often singled out students who excelled. Jimmy was one of her favorites. She gave him extra assignments and reading lists. She awarded him a silver star for every five books he read, and a gold star for every ten. When he was in the fifth grade, Miss Coleman suggested that Jimmy read *War and Peace* by Russian author Leo Tolstoy. At first, Jimmy thought it was about cowboys and Indians. He soon discovered that *War and Peace* told the story of a war between France and Russia in the early 1800s. The novel is more than 1400 pages long. Even so, Jimmy took pride in reading every single page.

Jimmy's parents encouraged reading at home too. When the children were small, Mr. Earl sat in his easy chair in front of the fireplace and read aloud. His own reading included newspapers, magazines, and farming journals.

Jimmy's mother read constantly. As soon as the children learned to read on their own, she encouraged them to bring their books to dinner. After saying the blessing, everyone opened their books and began reading. Talking was forbidden. Years later, when he became a dad, Jimmy continued this practice with his own children.

The outdoor life

By the time Jimmy was eight years old, he did many chores on the farm. Mr. Earl grew cotton, sugar cane, and peanuts, as well as vegetables like sweet potatoes, okra, peas, corn, cabbage, turnips, and collards. Jimmy's most dreaded chore was mopping cotton. To do this, he brushed a mixture of arsenic, molasses, and water onto each cotton plant with a cloth mop. The sticky brown poison killed the bugs that ate the cotton, but it also attracted flies and honeybees. The flies and bees followed Jimmy and his mop through the cotton field. Flies stuck to the bucket. By the time Jimmy got home, his pants were so stiff with the sticky mix that they would stand up by themselves in a corner of his bedroom.

There were plenty of breaks from farm work. Hunting and fishing were part of everyday life in rural Georgia too. By the time Jimmy was six, his father had taught him how to shoot a gun. He began with a BB gun and moved up to a Remington .22 semiautomatic rifle. Jimmy joined his dad hunting doves and bobwhite quail.

Jimmy was the best tree-climber in all of Archery, and sometimes, when the farmers went **possum** hunting, they invited Jimmy along. During possum hunts, he climbed high into the trees and shook the branches, knocking the possum to the ground. The men on the ground tried to capture it before the dogs did.

Jimmy and his dad were fascinated with the lives of Native Americans. They often hiked in the fields or streams around Archery looking for Native American pottery, arrowheads, or spearheads. Winter was the best time to find such things because rain often washed long-buried items to the surface. When they did discover a bit of pottery or an arrowhead, Jimmy and his dad would study it for hours before adding it to their collection. Hunting, fishing, and searching for arrowheads became lifelong hobbies.

Chapter 3

Black and White Worlds

Archery was home to dozens of African-American farmers and railroad workers. Their homes were scattered throughout the surrounding countryside. Most of the farmers worked for Mr. Earl. Their sons were Jimmy's playmates. Jimmy's best friend, A.D. Davis, was about the same age as Jimmy. A.D. lived with his aunt and uncle. They didn't know exactly when A.D. had been born, so A.D. adopted Jimmy's birthday, October 1, as his own. That way, the boys could celebrate together.

A.D., like almost all of Jimmy's playmates, was black. Jimmy and his friends worked hard. They played hard too. They played baseball, climbed trees, and went fishing. The boys made many of their own toys. They made kites and flips, which are slingshots. To make flips the boys attached big rubber bands to forked sticks. They used rocks or corncobs for ammunition. After reading

Jimmy spent summer days outside, without shirt or shoes.

Courtesy of the Jimmy Carter Library

an article in *Boys' Life* magazine, Jimmy and his friends made popguns out of rubber bands, clothespins, and wood. They spent hours throwing homemade spears or rolling the steel hoops that came with the wooden kegs used on the farm.

From early March to late October, Jimmy rarely wore shoes. Wet dirt squished between his toes as he raced through muddy fields. He went to school barefoot, too, although he used care to avoid splinters when crossing the school's wooden floors. Other dangers—briars, nails, or rusty barbed wire—lurked outdoors. Even so, Jimmy loved the freedom of going without shoes or a shirt whenever he could.

Rachel Clark

Jimmy's mother was often away, working many hours each day as a nurse. Jimmy later wrote, "The strong memory in my mind is coming home and my mother not being there." Instead, Jimmy was greeted by Rachel Clark. Rachel cooked for the family and cared for Jimmy and his sisters. Rachel was one of the most important people in Jimmy's life. In 1995, he published a book of poems, *Always a Reckoning, and Other Poems.* The first poem in the collection is called "Rachel." Jimmy writes:

> *My young life, shaped by those I loved,*
> *Felt the gentle touch of Rachel Clark...*

He goes on to write that Rachel was not only a hard worker, but that she had a graceful way about her that reminded Jimmy of an African queen.

Rachel was married to Jack Clark, one of the supervisors on Mr. Earl's farm. Jack often decided which fields should be plowed and assigned workers to do the job. He worked around the barn, doing odd jobs and caring for the animals. Jimmy spent many hours with Jack Clark. It was Jack who taught Jimmy to hunt raccoons.

Whenever Jimmy's parents went away, he stayed with the Clarks. Rachel and Jack slept in the only bedroom. Jimmy slept on the floor on a narrow mattress filled

Courtesy of the Jimmy Carter Library

Jimmy thought of Rachel Clark as a second mother.

with corn shucks or straw. On cold nights, he dragged his mattress nearer the fireplace. Even when his parents were home, Jimmy often ate supper with the Clarks or joined them for games of cards or checkers. The Clarks' own children were grown and gone.

Bozo

Whenever Jimmy and A.D. went squirrel hunting, they took Jimmy's dog Bozo along. Jimmy, A.D., and Bozo made a great team. Bozo was the best squirrel-hunting dog in Archery, and when he spotted a squirrel in a tree, he'd begin barking. The frightened squirrel moved as far away from the dog as possible. That gave the boys a chance to circle around the tree, find the squirrel, and take it down.

Hunting wasn't just sport in Archery. It provided food for hungry farm families. So did fishing. When it was too wet to work in the fields, Jimmy and his friends would camp out near the muddy creek and spend the night fishing. They tied a fishhook on a string and tied that to poles they cut from trees along the bank. They used liver for bait, and then they placed the poles about a foot deep in the water. Every hour or so during the night, they checked the pole by lantern light. If any fish or eels had been tempted by the bait, they retrieved them. Eels had to be eaten fresh, so the boys cooked the eels over an open campfire and gobbled them up. The boys had to be careful, though, because poisonous snakes like water moccasins lived

Courtesy of the Jimmy Carter Library

Twelve-year-old Jimmy was proud of Bozo.

in the same waters as the eels and in the tree limbs overhead.

Segregation

Even as a child, Jimmy recognized the differences between his life and that of his black friends. He was much richer than his black neighbors. His home was larger and nicer. He owned expensive clothes and shoes (even though he didn't wear them much of the time). He owned a bike, a horse, and a baseball glove. Although Miss Lillian allowed Jimmy's black friends to eat with Jimmy in the Carter kitchen, his father was much more strict. For example, Jimmy's best friend, A.D., was not allowed to play tennis with Jimmy on Mr. Earl's court because of his skin color.

Life in Georgia was **segregated**. Whites and blacks generally did not mix at school, church, or social events. Jimmy's black friends went to separate schools and churches. Their houses were smaller and poorer than Jimmy's. Many of Archery's black families ate only two meals a day. Most meals consisted of cornbread spread with molasses and fatback (a cut of pork that is mostly fat). Some families had small gardens where they grew their own vegetables. None of these families could afford bicycles or radios.

Bishop Johnson

Most of the African-American men Jimmy knew when he was a boy were farm workers. They had neither money nor power. Bishop William Dexter Johnson was different. He was both wealthy and powerful. Bishop Johnson, who led the African Methodist Episcopal (AME) churches in five midwestern states, traveled throughout the world. He ran a private school, an insurance company, and a publishing firm whose headquarters were in Archery. Once a year, when he returned to his home base in Archery, he invited the Carters to attend services at St. Mark Church. The church overflowed with worshippers. A visiting choir sang, and Bishop Johnson preached. Jimmy knew the words to the hymns, but he wasn't always able to follow the swaying rhythms of the black congregation. However, once Bishop Johnson began preaching, Jimmy forgot—at least for a little while—that he was a white boy in a black church. As he later wrote, "the sense of being brothers and sisters in Christ wiped away any thoughts of racial differences."

When Bishop Johnson wanted to speak with Mr. Earl, he arrived in a chauffer-driven limousine. The chauffer would blow the horn, and Mr. Earl would step outside to speak with the Bishop. The men laughed and talked together, but Bishop Johnson never entered the Carter house. Doing so would have broken the rules of Georgia's segregated society.

Bishop Johnson died when Jimmy was twelve. The Bishop's funeral was the largest that the people of Archery had ever seen. The parade of cars extended for over a mile. Many had out-of-state license plates. Most of those who attended the funeral were black, but Miss Lillian went, and she took Jimmy along. Mr. Earl stayed home. Jimmy began to realize that his father was not as open-minded and accepting as his mother. As time went on, Jimmy adopted his mother's belief that all people of all races should be treated with love and respect.

Growing apart

Once in a while, Jimmy and A.D. went to Americus to see a movie. They boarded the train in Archery. Both paid fifteen cents, but Jimmy rode in the seats marked "White," while A.D. sat in the seats marked "Colored." Once they reached the theater, Jimmy bought his ticket at the front entrance and took a seat downstairs or in the first balcony. A.D. purchased a ticket at the back door and sat in the third level balcony, farthest from the screen. They went home together, eagerly discussing the movie. At the time, Jimmy never questioned the forced separation of whites and blacks; he accepted it as the way things were done.

One day, when Jimmy was about fourteen, everything changed. As the boys approached a gate, Jimmy was surprised when A.D. opened it and stood back to let Jimmy pass through. At first he thought it was a trick. Later, he wrote, "It was a small act, but a deeply symbolic one." From that time on, his black friends no longer treated him like an equal. They treated Jimmy more like they treated his father, not as a friend, but as if he was in charge. The boys were moving toward their adult roles in separate black and white worlds. Jimmy began spending more time with his classmates in Plains and less time with his childhood pals.

Chapter 4

Growing Up

Jimmy's relationship to his black friends was not the only change that occurred around the time Jimmy entered the eighth grade. His faith changed too. Every Sunday since Jimmy was very young, Mr. Earl fixed breakfast before taking Jimmy and his sisters to church. He sent them to their own classes while he taught a Sunday school class for older boys. When Jimmy was nine, he moved into his father's class. Jimmy attended Sunday school, memorized Bible verses, and listened to the preacher. For one week each summer, the church held a **revival**. The revival was a series of church services designed to renew the community's faith. Each evening, visiting preachers gave powerful sermons. At the end of the sermon, the preacher asked nonmembers to step forward and accept Christ as their Savior. Jimmy was eleven when he stepped forward. The following Sunday, he was baptized along with other new church members.

At first, Jimmy believed everything he was taught in Sunday school and church. But by the time he was thirteen, he began to have doubts. He believed that God created the universe, and that Jesus Christ was God's son. He believed that Christ had died for his sins. But he had trouble accepting Christ's promise that all believers would receive eternal life. How could that be possible? Jimmy was afraid that death would separate him from the people he loved most—his mother and father. At the end of every prayer, he silently added the words, "And, God, please help me believe in the resurrection."

Jimmy (bottom right) is shown here with some of his classmates at Plains High School.

Jimmy thought he was the only person with doubts, and he was filled with guilt and loneliness. As he got older, prayer and Bible study eased his doubts, and his faith grew stronger.

Planning for the future

Jimmy worried about his future on earth too. From the time he was six, his goal had been to attend the Naval Academy in Annapolis, Maryland. He wanted to serve in the navy, like his uncle, Tom Gordy. "He was my distant hero," Jimmy later wrote. "Through all the years of my boyhood, he and I wrote letters back and forth, mine giving news about the family and his coming from the far reaches of the Pacific Ocean and filled with information about the exotic places his ships were visiting." Jimmy taped Uncle Tom's postcards to his bedroom walls. One of Jimmy's prized possessions was a three-foot model of a ship. He imagined himself sailing it across the ocean. At the time, he'd never even seen an ocean.

Jimmy wrote to the Naval Academy for a catalog. When it arrived, he studied the entrance requirements. Getting into the Naval Academy was going to be difficult. Jimmy worried that he was not tall enough, that his teeth didn't meet perfectly, and that his feet were too flat. But Jimmy never lost sight of his goal. He read books about the navy and got excellent grades in school. However, to get into a military academy, he would need a special appointment from a congressman. That might not happen no matter how tall he grew or how many As he earned on his report card.

So Jimmy prepared for life as a farmer just in case his dream of going to Annapolis fell through. He joined the Future Farmers of America (FFA). He learned woodworking, blacksmithing, welding, and furniture making. He learned how to care for animals, crops, and farm equipment. The FFA held speaking competitions, as well as animal judging contests. Jimmy excelled. Eventually, he became one of the club's officers.

Setting goals

Jimmy set difficult goals for himself. He expected to get excellent grades, excel at sports, and develop good mental habits. When he began the eighth grade in Plains, he wrote the following list:

Good Mental Habits

If you think in the right way, you will develop:

1. *The habit of accomplishing what you attempt.*
2. *The habit of expecting to like other people.*
3. *The habit of deciding quickly what you'd like to do and doing it.*
4. *The habit of sticking to it.*
5. *The habit of welcoming cheerfully all wholesome ideas and experiences.*
6. *A person who wants to build good mental habits should avoid the idle daydream, should give up worry and anger; hatred and envy; should neither fear nor be ashamed of anything that is honest and purposeful.*

At the all-white Plains High School, Jimmy applied these "Good Mental Habits." Miss Coleman, the school superintendent, expected a good deal of all her students, whether they planned to become navy officers, farmers, or secretaries. She expected even more of Jimmy. He memorized Bible verses and poetry, took part in spelling bees and writing contests, listened to the music of world-renowned composers, and studied the paintings of famous artists. Miss Coleman held classroom debates on important issues of the day. Jimmy joined the debating team and competed against other schools.

Sports were a part of Jimmy's school life too. The school's baseball season occurred during spring planting. Mr. Earl needed Jimmy on the farm, so he couldn't join the team, but he played pickup games every chance he got. In winter, Jimmy played basketball. His teammates called him "Peewee" because he was the shortest on the team, but he was also the quickest. Jimmy's speed led him to victory as a member of the school's track team, too, and during his last two years of high school, he made the varsity basketball team.

Jimmy spent more and more time in Plains. The church held parties for children and teens. At first, Jimmy rode his bike to church events, but by the time he was twelve, his father let him drive to town for Sunday night meetings of the Baptist Young People's Union (BYPU). Georgia did not require driver's licenses until 1940, so Jimmy, like many farm boys, had learned to drive trucks and tractors around the farm. When Mr. Earl let Jimmy drive his pickup to town, he told Jimmy to go directly to the event and to return home as soon as it ended.

The church sponsored "pound parties" in private homes throughout Plains. Each person brought a pound of refreshments. That way, there was plenty to eat. Jimmy and his friends danced and visited while parents kept watch. The most popular dance of the day was the jitterbug, a kind of swing dance with lots of turns, spins, and lifts. The boys liked to twirl their partners and create complicated new steps. At "pound parties," teens were required to switch partners often so that everyone had a chance to dance. Jimmy had lots of girlfriends, but he vowed that he wouldn't say "I love you" until he met the girl he intended to marry. It was a vow he kept.

Chapter 5

War and Peace

Sunday afternoon, December 7, 1941, seventeen-year-old Jimmy Carter was home alone listening to music on the radio. Suddenly, the music stopped. An announcer came on. "We interrupt this program to bring you a special news bulletin. The Japanese have attacked Pearl Harbor, Hawaii, by air ..."

Like all Americans, Jimmy was shocked. He wasn't sure where Pearl Harbor was located. What did this attack mean? When his family returned home, Jimmy discussed the news with his father. They learned that Japanese bombs had killed over two thousand servicemen. Another thousand were wounded in the attack. The next day, Jimmy and his father listened as President Roosevelt asked Congress to declare war between the United States and Japan. The United States had officially entered World War II.

A few days later, the Carters received word that Jimmy's uncle, Tom Gordy, had been captured by the Japanese on the Pacific Island of Guam. That news brought the war even closer to Plains. Everyone prayed that Tom would make it home.

Meanwhile, America prepared for war. The United States was fighting in Europe against the Germans and the Italians, and in Asia against the Japanese. Several of Jimmy's high school classmates joined the army or the navy. Jimmy did not sign up. He planned to serve his country as a navy officer after he graduated from Annapolis. The navy would need good officers like him in the difficult times ahead.

Jimmy (bottom right) posed with his high school graduating class in 1941.

Mr. Earl spoke with the district congressman, Steven Pace, about Jimmy's going to Annapolis. Congressman Pace suggested that Jimmy begin college, and maybe, in another year, he would consider appointing him to Annapolis. So Jimmy began classes at Georgia Southwestern College in Americus. He did so well in chemistry that the professor gave him a part-time job as a lab assistant. He finished the year with excellent grades, but Congressman Pace failed to appoint him to Annapolis. Jimmy began to doubt that he would ever get into Annapolis. He switched to Georgia Tech in Atlanta to study engineering. Finally, in 1943, Congressman Pace appointed Jimmy to Annapolis.

Annapolis

In June, Jimmy boarded a train for Annapolis, Maryland. Like other midshipmen, Jimmy took classes in seamanship, navigation, astronomy, engineering, and naval plans and procedures. He took a special course in identifying ships and planes. When the outlined image of a ship or plane was flashed onto a screen for a fraction of a second, he could recognize it. He also learned to fly seaplanes, which take off and land on the water.

Each summer the midshipmen trained for battle on older battleships. These training missions were dangerous because the war continued in Europe. German submarines patrolled the ocean, ready to attack enemy ships. Jimmy was assigned to the USS *New York*, an ancient battleship. He did everything from scrubbing the decks—and the toilets—to manning an anti-aircraft gun. He wore a life jacket at all times and slept on the deck near his anti-aircraft gun station in case of attack.

Rosalynn

At the end of summer, Jimmy returned to Plains on a short leave from the naval academy. His sister Ruth introduced him to her best friend, Rosalynn Smith. Rosalynn had been admiring the photo of Jimmy that hung on Ruth's wall. She thought he was the handsomest young man she had ever seen. Jimmy liked Rosalynn, too, and invited her to go to a movie. When he returned home that night, he told his mother that he had met the girl he wanted to marry.

Like Jimmy, Rosalynn was born in Plains and attended Plains High School. She was active in church and attended the same summer revival services that Jimmy did. The revivals made an impression. She later wrote, "God was a real presence in my life."

Rosalynn, who is three years younger than Jimmy, studied hard in school and earned good grades. When she was in the third grade, the teacher asked her to help teach the second-graders who were having trouble in math. It was an honor. Rosalynn dreamed of faraway places as she read books like *Heidi*, *Hans Brinker*, and *Robinson Crusoe*. When she was in seventh grade, she won a prize of five dollars for getting the highest grades in the class. That would be more than seventy-seven dollars today!

Rosalynn was only thirteen when her father became seriously ill. Jimmy's mother, Miss Lillian, often stopped by the house to help nurse Rosalynn's father.

Jimmy and Rosalynn pose for a wedding photo.

One day, Mr. Smith called Rosalynn and her brothers to his bedside. He explained that he was not going to get well. "You are good children," he said, "and I'm depending on you to be strong." He told the children that he wanted each of them to go to college. It was a promise that Rosalynn intended to keep. Her father died soon after, and Rosalynn worked hard both at school and helping her mother at home. However, as soon as she graduated from high school, she began attending Georgia State College for Women.

Good news

Rosalynn had finished her first year of college when she met Jimmy. A few weeks later, on August 6, 1945, the United States dropped an atomic bomb on Hiroshima, Japan. The bomb flattened the city and killed more than a hundred thousand Japanese people. Three days later, the US bombed another Japanese city, Nagasaki, killing tens of thousands more. Jimmy was on board a ship with hundreds of other sailors. They sat on the deck and listened as President Truman spoke over the ship's radio. He described the atomic bomb that had been dropped on Japan. Jimmy later wrote about the experience, "There was no way to understand the meaning of the **nuclear weapons** used in the attack on two Japanese cities."

Soon after the bombing, Japan surrendered. World War II was over. People across the country rejoiced. In Plains, church bells rang and people gathered to pray. Rosalynn thanked God that Jimmy would not have to go to war.

The Carters received more good news. Tom Gordy, Jimmy's favorite uncle who had been reported captured and then dead, was found alive. During the war, the Japanese had forced him to work on a mountain railroad system. He'd been beaten and starved. But he recovered quickly once he was treated in an American military hospital. He lived many more years—long enough to see Jimmy elected governor of Georgia.

Jimmy received more good news when Rosalynn agreed to marry him. They were married on July 7, 1946, in Plains. Only their families and a few close friends attended. Right afterward, Jimmy and Rosalynn left Plains to begin their life together in Norfolk, Virginia. A year later, their first child, John William Carter, was born. They called him "Jack."

Atomic submarines

In 1948, when Jimmy's assignment on the USS *Wyoming* was coming to an end, he applied for submarine school. The navy's submarine service selects officers who are smart, dependable, calm, and able to make good decisions quickly. Submariners must be in top physical condition. Jimmy fit the description perfectly.

In submarine school, Jimmy learned how to operate a submarine. Rescue drills took place in a giant water tank. In one exercise, students entered the tank through the bottom and swam up through one hundred feet of water to the surface. That's like climbing a ten-story building!

After Jimmy graduated from submarine school, he was sent to Hawaii. Life in Hawaii suited the Carters. Jimmy learned to play the ukulele, a kind of Hawaiian guitar, and Rosalynn danced the hula. She made bright floral shirts for Jimmy, little Jack, and the new baby, James Earl Carter III. They called the baby Chip. A third son, Donnel Jeffrey, called "Jeff," was born two years later after the Carters had moved to Connecticut.

Jimmy's navy crewmates called him "Jim." They said he was smart, organized, and serious. He later wrote about his life in submarines: "We would stay submerged for long periods of time, working in stockinged feet. We would hear all kinds of strange sea-creature sounds and could detect ships at extraordinary distances."

Jimmy, eager for a new challenge, applied to work in the navy's new nuclear submarine program. He learned everything he could about **nuclear energy**. The work fascinated him, and he put all his determination into preparing to become the engineering officer and learning how to operate the navy's new nuclear submarine, the *Seawolf*. A call from home changed everything. Jimmy never sailed with the *Seawolf*.

Chapter 6

Return to Plains

The phone rang. It was Miss Lillian with terrible news: Mr. Earl was dying of cancer. Jimmy got permission from his commander to return to Plains. He spent hours at his father's bedside. They talked about old times. Jimmy told his father about the navy. Friends and neighbors dropped by with food and flowers.

Jimmy later wrote, "A surprising number wanted to recount how my father's personal influence, community service, and many secret acts of generosity had affected their lives." The stories amazed Jimmy. They made him wonder whether he should stay in the navy or return to Plains and follow his father's example of helping the community. As he drove back to his navy base, he made a big decision. He would leave the navy and return to Plains to take over his father's business, Carter's Warehouse.

Jimmy was determined to go home, but Rosalynn loved navy life. Her protests did not convince Jimmy to change his mind. Jeff was a baby, Chip was three, and Jack was in the first grade when the Carters returned to Georgia.

Peanut farmer

Jimmy worked hard to try to rebuild Mr. Earl's peanut business. He worked long hours doing heavy work all by himself weighing tons of peanuts, determining their quality, and selling them to other businesses. The peanuts would be made into peanut butter, peanut candy, or peanut oil. Eventually, Rosalynn took over as bookkeeper and business manager. The boys helped out too. They weeded the rows of peanut plants and attached labels to bags of seeds. Everyone helped make the business a success.

The Carters found time to have fun too. They rented a big house on the edge of town. They boys had a pony and dogs. They caught frogs, bugs, pigeons, lizards, and snakes. Some people in town said the house was haunted, so the boys searched for ghosts. They never found any, of course, but one day Jack discovered a secret room between a bedroom ceiling and the attic floor. There was even a ladder that the boys could use to reach their secret hideaway. Why was it there? They talked about it for hours and dreamed up all kinds of silly answers.

Jimmy, who had always loved being outdoors, took his sons fishing and camping. On weekends, they often drove four hours to Panama City Beach in Florida to go

Jimmy pulls peanut vines in one of his fields.

fishing and boating. One year the family took a camping trip around Georgia, spending each night of the week at a different state park. Another year, they took a two-week camping trip to North Carolina, South Carolina, Virginia, Delaware, and Washington, DC. When they stopped in Annapolis, Maryland, Jimmy showed the boys around his old school, the United States Naval Academy.

Plunging into politics

In 1954, the United States Supreme Court made one of its most important rulings, one that touched all Americans. At the time, the laws in seventeen states, including Georgia, required elementary schools to be segregated. This meant that white children went to one school and black children went to another. The Supreme Court ruling overturned those laws and required that schools become **integrated**. That meant that children of all races would attend school together. People through-out the South feared that the ruling would change their lives forever.

Many southern communities responded to the 1954 Supreme Court decision by forming the White Citizens' Council. In Plains, the chief of police and the railroad station agent were the leaders. They asked Jimmy to join them, but he refused. A few days later they returned. This time, they told Jimmy that every other white man in town had joined the White Citizens' Council. Jimmy Carter still said *no*. The next time the leaders visited, they brought several of Jimmy's friends and customers with them. The members of the White Citizens' Council offered to pay the five dollars dues for him. Cost wasn't the issue. Jimmy supported integration. His childhood friends had been black, and he had served with many black sailors in the navy. Like his mother, Jimmy wanted his

Courtesy of the Jimmy Carter Library

This 1960 family photo shows Chip (left) and Jeff (right) helping their dad on the peanut farm.

African-American neighbors to be treated fairly and given equal opportunities.

Despite threats to his business, Jimmy held firm. A few customers refused to do business with Carter's Warehouse. Jimmy was harassed and the boys were teased at school. Chip, who was in grade school, learned the hard way that the family had been kicked out of the Americus

Country Club, an all-white golf club. One day when his mom dropped him off for a golf lesson, he was not allowed to go inside or to take his lesson. Chip had to wait on the curb for over two hours until his mother returned.

In 1956, Jimmy Carter joined the county school board. He began to see firsthand one of the reasons why the Supreme Court ruled that segregated schools cheat black students.

He wrote later, "It seems hard to believe now, but I was actually a member of the county school board for several months before it dawned on me that white children rode buses to their school and black students walked to theirs."

No one had ever mentioned it—not the black parents nor the white. He came to see that the schools—and the education they provided—were *not* equal. Black teachers had less training and earned less money than white teachers. Black children often used old textbooks that had been thrown away by white schools. Schools for black children were in poor condition. The more he learned, the more troubled Jimmy became. He tried to improve the situation in the black schools, but integration was years away. When the Civil Rights Act was passed in 1964, only two Southern states—Tennessee and Texas—had more than two percent of their black students attending integrated schools.

Entering politics

In 1961, the Carters built a new brick ranch house near the center of Plains. Jimmy was a well-respected businessman. He and Rosalynn were active in the community. On the morning of his thirty-eighth birthday, Jimmy surprised Rosalynn when he announced that he was going to run for the Georgia State Senate. Little did he know he was on his way to becoming president of the United States.

Rosalynn was thrilled. She supported Jimmy's goals even though it meant that she would handle the business—and the boys—alone during the time that Jimmy was in Atlanta attending the legislature.

First Jimmy had to win the Democratic **primary**. He ran against Homer Moore, who ran a farm supply business. If Jimmy won the primary, he would run in a general election against the Republican **candidate**.

Jimmy made posters, advertised in local newspapers, and called on supporters. He shook hands with shoppers, farmers, and businessmen. Rosalynn called voters on the telephone and helped Jimmy's sister Gloria mail thousands of letters asking people to vote for Jimmy Carter. Whenever he could, Jimmy convinced local radio announcers to interview him. He made one TV appearance on the night before the primary.

On Election Day, Jimmy drove to each of the voting places. It looked as if he was going to win. Then he got a call from Quitman County, the smallest county in his district. John Pope, one of Jimmy's friends, had been watching the voting there. He noticed that Joe Hurst, a local politician, threatened anyone who voted for Jimmy Carter. When one elderly couple voted for Carter, Hurst pulled their ballots out of the box, tore them up, and

JIMMY **CARTER**

FOR STATE SENATOR

Courtesy of the Jimmy Carter Library

Jimmy hoped his campaign posters would attract votes.

said, "If I ever catch you voting wrong again, I'm gonna burn your house down." The threats worked. At the end of the day, Jimmy Carter lost the election.

Jimmy fumed. He hated losing. But he hated unfair elections even more. Jimmy believes that leaders must be elected fairly or people won't trust them. Democracies depend on fair elections. Jimmy went to Quitman County and questioned the voters. Many admitted that they had been threatened. Jimmy discovered that 420 ballots had been placed in the Quitman County ballot box. But the county only had 333 registered voters! The voters had been cheated, and so had Jimmy Carter. He took the story to the newspapers, radio, and television stations. In November, a judge ruled that the Quitman County votes would not count. He declared Jimmy Carter the winner of the primary.

Jimmy won the general election too. He served in the Georgia State Senate from 1962 to 1966. He read every bill before he voted on it. That was a lot of reading! The Senate voted on eight hundred to one thousand bills each year or as many as twenty-two bills per day. Jimmy took a speed-reading course to keep up. He arrived for work early and stayed late. He wanted to do his best, just like he had in the navy. His hard work won him the respect of other Georgia lawmakers. In 1965, they named him one of the five most respected state senators in Georgia. Jimmy enjoyed politics so much that he decided to run for the United States Congress in the next election.

Chapter 7

Losing an Election and Finding Faith

When Jimmy began campaigning for the United States Congress, he felt he had a good chance to win. So did his friends and advisors. But in May 1966, the Democratic candidate for governor had a heart attack. Jimmy tried to convince others to run for governor, but no one seemed interested. It was going to be a tough race. Finally, Jimmy realized that he was the most likely candidate. He quit the race for Congress and ran for governor instead.

Jimmy crossed the state giving speeches and shaking hands. He tried to remember the names of everyone he met. As soon as he returned to his car after an event, he repeated all the names he remembered into a small tape recorder. He added a comment about each person to help jog his memory. Over time, he developed a great memory for names.

In 1966, the family helped Jimmy campaign. In this photo, Jeff (left) and his brother Jack (back) help their mother, Rosalynn, distribute pamphlets.

When he returned home, Rosalynn and his sister Gloria used the names to write letters asking the voters to support Jimmy. Friends and family helped in other ways too. Jimmy's brother Billy managed Carter's Warehouse while Jimmy campaigned. Sons Jack and Chip crossed the state meeting with voters. Jeff, who was thirteen, traveled with Rosalynn. So did Miss Lillian. They returned home every Saturday, attended church Sunday, and then returned to campaigning on Monday. Jimmy, his family, and his friends shook hands, distributed handouts, and appeared on local radio and TV shows. By Election Day, Jimmy and Rosalynn had shaken hands with over 300,000 people.

But the effort wasn't enough. Jimmy Carter lost the election. He also lost weight and $66,000 of their family's savings. It was a terrible defeat. The Carters were sick with disappointment, but after a few days, they returned to work and school and tried to put the loss behind them.

Ruth's advice

Six weeks after the election, Jimmy's sister Ruth came to visit. Now married to a veterinarian, Robert Stapleton, and living in North Carolina, Ruth had become a well-known Christian author and preacher. As Ruth and Jimmy walked in the woods, he shared his disappointment at losing the election. "God has rejected me through the people's vote," he said.

Ruth disagreed. "You have to believe that out of this defeat can come a greater life," she said. She quoted from James 1:2: "Consider it pure joy, my brothers and sisters, whenever you face trials of many kinds." Ruth encouraged Jimmy to develop a closer relationship with Jesus and to accept God's will, "No matter what he should want you to do."

After the conversation with Ruth, Jimmy spent more time studying the Bible and trying to understand what God wanted of him. A few weeks later, his pastor posed a question to the congregation. If you were arrested for being a Christian, would there be enough evidence to convict you? Jimmy pondered the question for weeks. Later he wrote, "I finally decided that if arrested and charged with being a committed follower of God, I could probably talk my way out of it." For Jimmy, that was a disturbing thought!

As a Baptist deacon, he visited families in Plains who did not attend church. He invited them to come to worship. In the previous fourteen years he had visited 140 people. He felt proud of that record until he remembered that during his recent political campaign, he had visited 300,000 people on his own behalf. What had he done for God? It was time to put his skills to work on behalf of the church. Jimmy joined a Southern Baptist program called Project 500, which hoped to establish five hundred new churches, and switched from campaigning for himself to campaigning for Jesus Christ.

Around the same time, Miss Lillian announced that she was joining the Peace Corps. At age sixty-seven, Miss Lillian, went to India and worked as a nurse at a small clinic.

Another surprise came in early 1967 when Rosalynn learned she was pregnant. The Carters had always wanted more children, and the boys, then twenty, seventeen, and fifteen, hoped for a sister. They even picked out a name—Amy. Their wish was granted. Amy Lynn Carter was born on October 19, 1967.

Working for Jesus

Amy wasn't the only miracle in Jimmy's life. She was six months old when Jimmy traveled to Pennsylvania to help establish a new Baptist church in Lock Haven. "The whole week was almost a miracle to me," Jimmy wrote, "I felt the presence of God's influence in my life. I felt then, and ever since, that each individual person I meet is important to me."

Jimmy seized other opportunities to witness to his faith. He traveled to Springfield, Massachusetts, and worked with Pastor Cruz, a Spanish-speaking pastor from Cuba. Using the Spanish he had learned in the navy, Jimmy worked with recent immigrants. Jimmy listened when Pastor Cruz told a group of children the story of Jesus raising Lazarus from the dead. Jimmy was amazed at the children's response. They clapped, cheered, and jumped for joy. By the end of the week, forty-six people had accepted Christ, and they formed a new church. Elroy Cruz left a lasting impression on Jimmy when he said, "You need have only two loves. One for God, and one for the person who happens to be standing in front of you."

Another try

Jimmy had been planning to run for governor again ever since his conversation with his sister Ruth. He gathered a team of trusted advisors who raised money and developed ads. In 1970, Jimmy announced his plans. As governor of Georgia, he promised to improve the schools, obey the laws for integrating the schools, and fix the tax system. A room full of supporters cheered.

Many college students offered to help elect Jimmy Carter. They wanted the South to change. Like Jimmy, they favored integration. A few years earlier, when Chip Carter was a junior in Plains High School, two black students began attending classes. There were no protests. It was the kind of quiet change that was happening all over the South, and which Jimmy Carter supported.

Jimmy's campaign ads highlighted his life as a peanut farmer. One TV ad showed him working on the farm as an announcer said, "Jimmy Carter knows what it's like to work for a living. He still works twelve hours a day in his shirt sleeves on the farm at Plains during peanut harvest..." This earned him the support of working people who believed that a working man like Jimmy Carter could understand their problems. Jimmy spoke to farmers and factory workers. He stood outside shopping centers greeting shoppers. During the campaign, he gave 1,800 speeches in communities throughout Georgia.

The family helped campaign too. Amy, who was only two, stayed with Rosalynn's mother. Jack was in Vietnam serving with the United States Navy, so he couldn't help. Chip took a year off from college to campaign, and as soon as Jeff graduated from high school, he joined the effort. Seventy-two-year-old Miss Lillian campaigned almost every day. Rosalynn, Chip, Jeff, and Miss Lillian visited towns and cities all across Georgia. They went separately so that they could reach as many people as possible. They began their day wherever policemen, firemen, or garbage collectors gathered before work. They visited factories, stores, and special events.

Although they campaigned separately, Jimmy and Rosalynn worked as a team. During the campaign, they shook over 600,000 hands. That was half of the people of voting age living in Georgia. Rosalynn Carter went to sea in a shrimp boat, floated around in a hot-air balloon, and even attended a rattlesnake roundup. Wherever they went, they handed out brochures, shook hands, and urged people to elect Jimmy for governor.

In September 1970, Georgia's Democrats chose Jimmy Carter as their candidate for governor. That November, Jimmy won the election!

Chapter 8

Governor Carter

On January 12, 1971, Jimmy Carter was sworn in as governor of Georgia. The United States Naval Academy Band played, and an all-black choir sang the "Battle Hymn of the Republic." Several pastors offered prayers, and the bells of a nearby church chimed.

In Governor Carter's inauguration speech, he promised to improve the schools and make sure that taxes were fair. He surprised his audience when he said, "I say to you quite frankly that the time for racial **discrimination** is over." He promised that no "poor, rural, weak, or black person should be [kept from getting] an education, a job, or simple justice." Jimmy Carter believed that good government should provide for the needs of the people—all the people. The speech brought him lots of attention. A few months later, in 1971, *Time Magazine* wrote an article about the changes taking place in the South. They put

Jimmy Carter's picture on the cover and wrote a glowing report about his plans.

Governor Carter got right to work. When he became governor, there were only three African-Americans serving on state boards. By the time he left office, there were fifty-three. He increased the number of black state employees by over two thousand. He made it possible for African-Americans to join the state patrol, and he chose a black officer to serve in his security force. One time, he was invited to speak at a country club. The members there asked him not to bring the black officer with him, but when he arrived, the black state trooper was at his side. Jimmy then gave a speech against racism.

Jimmy worked long hours. Sometimes he read until 1:00 a.m., and then woke up early and left for his office at the statehouse. He followed news around the state and tried to solve problems before they got worse. During his first year in office, a conflict developed in Hancock County. A group of white citizens feared that the black county supervisor had too much power. Tension between the races increased. Soon, two groups, one white and one black, armed themselves with submachine guns, ready to fight.

At the time, many governors would have sent a large force of state troopers to Hancock. They might have even sent the National Guard. Not Jimmy. He believed in working things out quietly. He wanted both sides to talk about the situation and find a solution. He sent three men: a trusted advisor, a state patrolman, and an expert in solving conflicts. Two of the men were white; one was black. They had solved similar problems before.

This official photo shows Governor Carter in his office at the Georgia Capitol.

It took them three weeks to calm people down and remove the weapons, but they did it without a single shot being fired. The incident supported Jimmy's belief that problems could be solved peacefully.

Life in the governor's mansion

Jimmy loved his work, and his family enjoyed living in the governor's mansion in Atlanta. It was the first time in four years that the entire family lived together. Jack returned from the navy and began classes at Georgia Tech. Jeff and Chip attended Georgia State University. Amy, who was three, had a big bedroom next to her parents' room.

Soon after the Carters moved into the mansion, a young prisoner named Mary Prince arrived. Prison officials thought she might be a good nanny for Amy because Mary had experience taking care of children. In Georgia, it was the custom for prisoners to work in the governor's mansion as maids, cooks, and groundskeepers. Some of the prisoners had committed serious crimes, but they had earned the trust of prison officials. Mary had been accused of murder.

Would the Carters trust someone like that to take care of their precious child? They met with Mary, and they liked her. Jimmy later wrote, "Mary's intelligence and dedication convinced us to let her help Rosalynn care for Amy while I was governor." Amy trusted Mary too. She counted on Mary to care for her when her parents could not, and the two became close friends.

Mary came to love the Carters. "They always treated me like a part of the family even though I was in jail," she said. "They used to take me on trips, and he [Jimmy Carter] would say, 'She's a good friend, she's a friend of the family.'" When the Carters moved to the White House, Mary went along.

Working for the Carters changed Mary's life. She saw the Carters reading the Bible every morning and every night. She saw them pray and go to church. Eventually, she began going too. She accepted Christ and became a baptized member of the church.

Over time, the Carters learned why Mary was in prison. She had been visiting a small town when a man was murdered, and since she was the only visitor—and African-American—she was accused of the crime. Her lawyer had promised that if she admitted that she was guilty, she would get less time in jail. He was wrong. Mary was sentenced to life in prison. Eventually, Jimmy helped her contact the trial judge. When the judge re-opened the case, he found that Mary was not guilty after all. It took her many years to gain her freedom.

Today, Mary speaks about her experiences in front of large audiences. She wants people to understand how an innocent person can sometimes be found guilty. Jimmy Carter believes that Mary's case is a perfect example of how the American court system is often unfair to poor people, African-Americans, immigrants, and people with mental health problems. Mary continues to be a good friend to the Carters. In 2011, Jimmy said: "She [Mary] is a very wonderful person, and she's like a member of our own family. She's helped raise all of our children, all of our grandchildren, and all of our great grandchildren."

Thinking ahead

As governor, Jimmy spent his days making important decisions. He told a group of reporters that he prayed more as governor than he had ever prayed before. "I felt so heavily on my shoulders the decisions I made might very well affect many, many people."

Rosalynn Carter wanted to make a difference in people's lives too. She worked to improve mental hospitals and prisons throughout Georgia. She also supported the Special Olympics, a sports program for children with disabilities. At the governor's mansion, she managed banquets, organized arts programs, and entertained important guests. And, of course, she took care of the family.

While Jimmy was governor, he traveled throughout Georgia and the world. He rode Georgia's rivers in rafts, canoes, and kayaks. He visited state parks and studied the wildlife programs throughout the state. He designated land for several state parks along the Chattahoochee River, and he worked to preserve the coastline. When a new dam on the Flint River came up for a vote, he took two canoe trips along the river. It was a beautiful area, and Jimmy refused to approve the dam. Preserving the river for recreation was more important than building a dam. He also established the Georgia Heritage Trust to preserve more than two thousand historic places in Georgia.

He traveled the world in hopes of selling Georgia's products overseas and attracting new businesses to Georgia. Jimmy, Rosalynn, and several Georgia officials traveled to Mexico, Costa Rica, Colombia, Brazil, and Argentina. The trip was so successful that they planned another for the next year. This time they went to England, Belgium, and Germany. Jimmy and Rosalynn traveled to Israel. It was a chance to see places that they knew from reading the Bible. They had lunch in Nazareth, drove around the Sea of Galilee, visited Cana and Capernaum, and worshipped at Bethlehem where Jesus was born. They even swam in the Dead Sea. The travel was fun and educational. It also helped the state which opened trading offices in Germany, Belgium, Brazil, Canada, and Japan.

Chapter 9

Aiming High

Two years after Jimmy became governor, his advisors began asking him what he wanted to do next. At the time, Georgia law allowed a governor to serve only four years. His advisors said, "We think you should run for president." Jimmy had been thinking the same thing. He decided he was ready for the challenge, but he didn't announce his decision for another two years.

He began writing his autobiography, *Why Not the Best?* It was one way to introduce himself to America's voters. The autobiography began with stories of his boyhood in Archery and ended with his plans for the presidency. He also began studying subjects that he thought might help him as president: foreign affairs, the **economy**, energy, and American history. He read the biographies of past presidents to learn how to make good decisions and avoid bad ones.

Jimmy Carter's friendliness, honesty, and small-town values appealed to voters.

Once a month, Jimmy met with his advisors to discuss his campaign, but he didn't stop working as Georgia's governor. He knew that his record as a good governor would help him get elected. In a way, running for president made it easier for him to take bold steps. In February 1974, he hung a portrait of Martin Luther King Jr. in the state capitol building. Even though protestors marched outside, Jimmy joined the crowd inside the capitol singing "We Shall Overcome," a song to protest racial discrimination.

On December 16, 1974, Jimmy Carter stood in Atlanta before a crowd of three thousand cheering supporters and announced his decision to run for president. His campaign officially began when his term as governor ended on January 13, 1975.

In an early television interview, Jimmy said he enjoyed tackling difficult problems, and he talked about why he was running for president. Jimmy hoped to bring his values to government and to make the United States a nation of peace. He felt it was wrong to send troops into another country—unless that country was directly threatening the United States. "We don't have to show that we are strong. We *are* strong," Jimmy declared. "I want to see us once again have a nation that is as good and honest and decent and truthful and confident and compassionate and as filled with love as all the American people."

On the campaign trail

Jimmy's first goal was to win the Democratic Party Primary. He had eighteen months to convince the Democratic Party to choose him as their candidate for president. Unlike other candidates, who were still in office as senators or governors, Jimmy could spend all his time running for president. His family helped. They usually traveled separately so they could meet more people in distant places, like New Hampshire, Iowa, Florida, and South Dakota.

When Jimmy's oldest son, Jack, finished law school in June, he joined the campaign. So did his wife, Judy. However, Judy took a few weeks off in August to give birth to Jason, their first son, and Jimmy Carter's first grandson. At the time, Jimmy was in Boston appearing on a morning talk show. The show's host handed him a cigar and announced the birth to the world. Jimmy Carter was now a grandpa!

Campaigning in the 1970s was different from the way it is today. There were no cell phones, so it was not easy for the family to stay in touch. There was no Internet. No one could text or tweet or blog about their favorite candidate. Jimmy Carter couldn't conduct an interview on Facebook. Television news was limited to about thirty minutes a day. There were no twenty-four-hour-a-day television news channels. People relied on newspapers and radio.

Jimmy Carter and his family traveled by car, bus, train, and plane. They went to newspaper and radio stations, hoping to get interviewed. They stayed in the homes of ordinary people who had an extra room and were willing to share their supper. They stayed with rich and poor people in big cities and small towns. They got to know the problems facing all kinds of people in all kinds of places. What worried people? What did they expect their next president to do for them?

In 1975, Jimmy Carter stayed with fifty-one different families. Some of them were poor. Jimmy later said, "I was embarrassed when some people were so poor, to impose on them." But staying in homes built up a group of strong supporters in many states. They told their friends about Jimmy, and the friends told more friends. Support grew. After Jimmy was elected, he invited everyone who had hosted him or his family in their homes to come to the White House. Almost eight hundred people came! The Carters thanked them for their help and gave them small brass plaques: "A member of Jimmy Carter's family slept here."

On Saturday afternoons, the Carters returned to Plains and shared their experiences. They talked about what concerned the voters, and they made sure that they were all giving the same answers about important issues. Returning to Plains also gave Jimmy a much-needed break. Reporters got to see a different side of Jimmy Carter. One time, reporters watched him drain the dammed-up pond on his mother's property. Another time he played baseball with reporters and went fishing with Rosalynn.

During the presidential campaign, Jimmy started his day between four and five in the morning. He went to factories, stood by the door, and shook hands with workers leaving the night shift or beginning the day shift. He gave interviews on radio and TV and met with newspaper reporters. One supporter said, "Jimmy Carter outworked everyone. He's tireless." Carter himself said, "I can get up at nine and be rested or I can get up at six and be president."

New Hampshire

The New Hampshire primary happens early in the presidential race and gets lots of television and newspaper attention. Carter's supporters began to work early in New Hampshire. Chip Carter and his wife, Caron, moved to New Hampshire to campaign. They lived in a large house in Concord with lots of rooms for Carter volunteers. They called it Camp Carter.

Volunteers from Georgia paid their own expenses and went door-to-door telling people why Jimmy Carter deserved their support. No other candidate had ever done this sort of thing. People were amazed by the efforts of this group, who called themselves the Peanut Brigade. In one January week, the Peanut Brigade knocked on the doors of eighteen thousand Democratic households. The Peanut Brigade made a huge difference. Robert Curren, a New Hampshire Democrat commented, "If that many people thought that much about him to come all the way up here, then he must be a good man."

When Rosalynn arrived in New Hampshire, people greeted her carrying signs that said:

WIN WITH A GRIN

HEAL THE NATION WITH PEANUT OIL

PUT AMY'S DADDY IN THE WHITE HOUSE

LET'S CARTERIZE THE COUNTRY

WE LOVE YOU JIMMY AND ROSALYNN

Carter won in New Hampshire.

Chapter 10

Walking Humbly

Jimmy continued to win primary races. It looked as if he would become the Democratic Party's candidate. That meant that he needed to choose a running mate, someone to serve as vice president. He chose Walter Fritz Mondale, a senator from Minnesota. Mondale and Carter agreed on most issues, they liked each other, and they thought they could work well as a team. Senator Mondale knew how things were usually done in Washington. He wanted to be a new kind of vice president, one who would be more involved in running the country. He wanted an office in the West Wing of the White House near the president so that he could attend all major meetings and help make important decisions. Jimmy eagerly agreed. Since Jimmy was from the South, he felt that it was an advantage that Mondale came from the North. Together, they represented all the people. They were young, energetic, and willing to work hard.

The Carters went to New York in July for the Democratic National Convention. They attended parties and receptions, gave interviews, and invited five thousand Democratic delegates to a picnic. They served fried chicken, coleslaw, peanuts, and beer. Jimmy and Rosalynn shook hands for hours.

On the night he was chosen as the Democratic Party's candidate for president, Jimmy began his speech with these words, "My name is Jimmy Carter, and I'm running for president." Delegates cheered. Some even cried for joy. The Reverend Martin Luther King Sr., father of the great civil rights leader, gave a closing prayer. He said, "Surely the Lord sent Jimmy Carter to come on out and bring America back where she belongs." Then he led the delegates in singing "We Shall Overcome." It was a great beginning.

Convincing the voters

There were seventy-five days until the general election. The Carters returned to Georgia to rest—and to plan. Their lives would never be the same. Now that he was a candidate for president, the Secret Service protected Jimmy. Wherever he went, Secret Service men went with him. Newspaper reporters followed him, eager to hear what he had to say. Jimmy gave dozens of speeches and interviews all across the country. Now, everyone recognized Jimmy Carter.

They recognized Rosalynn too. She had always been shy, but campaigning had given her more confidence. She gave dozens of speeches, talked to newspaper reporters, and answered questions on the television show *Meet the Press*. It seemed as if everyone wanted to know more about the Carters.

Although black voters throughout the country and many Southern voters supported Jimmy Carter, many people outside of the South considered Carter too religious. He tried to explain that as a Baptist, he believed that the church and the government should remain separate. Jimmy followed Jesus's teaching in Mark 12:17: "Then Jesus said to them, 'Give back to Caesar what is Caesar's and to God what is God's.'" This means that in some areas, the government makes the rules, and in others, the church is in charge. In other words, people should pay taxes to the government, but the government should not require people to worship in any particular way. Jimmy found it difficult when people made comments about his faith, but he admitted, "The people have a right to know about the religious beliefs of their future president."

Jimmy was running against President Gerald Ford. As the election approached, the two candidates agreed to debate one another. Afterward, people argued about which candidate had done a better job. Jimmy felt that his performance made a difference and "gave the viewers reason to think that Jimmy Carter had something to offer," he said.

November 2, 1976, was Election Day. The Carters voted in Plains, and then they waited at an Atlanta hotel for the results to come in. It was three in the morning before they got the word. "We've won!" Jimmy shouted.

Preparing for Washington

It had been a close race. Jimmy Carter received 40.8 million votes to President Ford's 39.1 million. Jimmy later said, "I've never asked God to let me win an election or to let me have success in politics. I've just said, 'Lord, let my action be meaningful to you, and let the life that you've given me not be wasted.'"

The Carters spent the next few months planning for their move to Washington, DC. Jimmy and Rosalynn traveled to Washington to tour the White House. Rosalynn toured the family living quarters. That area of the White House is called "the mansion." Jimmy visited the Oval Office, which is in the West Wing where the president and his advisors work. The East Wing is reserved for the first lady and her staff. Rosalynn took photos to share with the family and to help plan for their move.

The first major event for any new president is the **inauguration** ceremony. Jimmy studied the speeches that earlier presidents had given at their inaugurations. Then he wrote his own speech. He chose to include a Bible verse from Micah 6:8. "He has shown you, O mortal, what is good. And what does the LORD require of you? To act justly and to love mercy and to walk humbly with your God." The verse described exactly what Jimmy Carter wanted to do as president. He wanted to do justice, show kindness, and honor God's commandments. It would not be easy.

Courtesy of the Jimmy Carter Library

The crowd cheered as the new president and his family walked from the Capitol to the White House in the inaugural parade.

Doing things differently

January 20, 1977, was Inauguration Day. At noon, Warren E. Burger, chief justice of the Supreme Court, **administered** the oath of office to Jimmy Carter. Jimmy used the same Bible that George Washington had used in 1789. He also made the same promise:

"I do solemnly swear (or affirm) that I will faithfully execute the office of president of the United States, and will to the best of my ability, preserve, protect and defend the Constitution of the United States."

After hugging his family and friends, he gave one of the shortest inaugural speeches ever. It lasted only eight minutes. He began with the words of Micah 6:8, and then he went on to list his plans to protect the rights of all people, create fair laws, and preserve the environment. He ended with these words: "When my time as your president has ended, I would hope that the nations of

Jimmy Carter was the first president who:
✓ walked in the inaugural parade
✓ came from Georgia
✓ graduated from the Naval Academy
✓ took the oath of office using his nickname

the world might say that we had built a lasting peace."

After the speech, it was time for the inaugural parade. The parade is a tradition going back to George Washington's time. Modern presidents ride in a shiny black limousine past waving crowds. Not Jimmy Carter. He got out of the car and began walking. At first, people along the parade route thought something was wrong with the car. But when they realized that the Carters had chosen to walk, they shouted, "They're walking! They're walking!" Jimmy and Rosalynn held hands as they walked the mile and a half to the White House. Nine-year-old Amy pranced and danced beside her parents.

Jimmy Carter later described it as one of the "few perfect moments in life when everything seems absolutely right." A newspaper reporter claimed it would be the thing most people would remember about Carter's inauguration. By walking to the White House Jimmy Carter showed people that he planned to do things differently. He wanted his presidency to be a new beginning for the United States.

Chapter 11

Doing Justice

While Jimmy found his way to the Oval Office, the rest of the family explored the White House. The main floor is open to tourists and is closely guarded by the secret service. The president's family lives on the second and third floors. Jimmy, Rosalynn, and Amy had bedrooms on the second floor. Jeff and Chip and their wives had rooms on the third floor. Son Jack and his wife, Judy, stayed in Georgia, where Jack worked as a lawyer.

The Carters did not change anything about the White House. They liked it the way it was. At first they treated the White House like a museum and were very careful not to disturb things. But they soon felt more at home. They tossed Frisbees in the yard. They went to the rooftop and watched the stars through Jeff's telescope. They bowled in the White House bowling alley and watched movies in the movie theater. It's nearly impossible for the president and his family to go bowling or to the movies without being mobbed, so having a bowling alley and a theater in the White House made life easier on everyone. After a while, the president built Amy a tree house in the backyard.

Amy

Four days after the inauguration, Amy began fourth grade at Thaddeus Stevens Elementary School, six blocks from the White House. Even before they arrived in Washington, the Carters had decided that Amy would attend public school. President Carter believed that the public schools suffered when good students switched to private schools. Even so, many newspapers reported that Amy would be attending a private school. The Carters held firm in sending Amy to public school, and they asked the reporters to give Amy some privacy.

However, on her first day of school, reporters and photographers crowded around her and nearly blocked her path. Amy was getting used to all the attention; she just kept walking. After the first day, the reporters agreed to focus on President and Mrs. Carter and to leave Amy out of the news.

It took a few days for Amy to feel at home in her new school. Stevens Elementary had 213 students. About half were black, and many were the children of workers at foreign embassies. Everyone was curious about the president's daughter. Not only was she the "new girl" in school, but Secret Service agents followed her everywhere. The children soon got used to having the Secret

Amy, shown here with Mary Prince, enjoyed life at the White House.

Service agents at school, and they began treating Amy like any other classmate. She made many friends and brought some of them to the White House to play. Mary Prince joined the family as Amy's nanny.

The family

In many ways, the Carters behaved like most families. They gathered together at supper each night to talk about issues of the day. Jimmy listened to what they said. After all, his wife and children were his strongest supporters. They were also his strongest critics. They told him the truth, even if they disagreed with his decisions. Amy helped by talking about her school. Her stories about school lunches and students who didn't speak English helped her dad understand problems facing students and teachers across the nation.

Rosalynn was Jimmy's partner in all things. They worked together in the White House just as they had at the peanut warehouse and during the many campaigns. They supported one another, sharing their hopes and their fears.

Jimmy wanted to keep his life as simple as possible— even in the White House. He asked the military band to stop playing "Hail to the Chief" whenever he entered a room. (In 1954, the Department of Defense had made this the official song used to announce the arrival of the United States president for events and ceremonies.) Jimmy preferred a simple spoken announcement, "Ladies and gentlemen, the president of the United States." It was certainly more humble, but people missed the music. After a few months, he asked the band to play on special occasions.

Keeping promises

Jimmy had a long list of promises he had made to voters during the campaign, and he didn't waste any time trying to keep them. Most mornings he woke at six, and as he entered the Oval Office, he recited the words of Psalm 19:14, "Let the words of my mouth and the meditation of my heart be acceptable in Thy sight, O Lord, my strength and my redeemer."

During his inaugural speech, Jimmy promised to promote human rights and keep peace throughout the world. As president, Jimmy encouraged world leaders to treat all people fairly, even those who disagreed with them. He wrote, "Human rights is the central concern of my administration." He convinced foreign leaders to free political prisoners and to allow people who were un-

> **What are human rights?**
> Human rights include the right to food, shelter, and education. The right to own property, to move from one country to another, and the right to a just trial are also basic human rights People should not have to fear being imprisoned unfairly or mistreated.

happy in one country to move to another. For example, Jimmy Carter persuaded leaders in the Soviet Union to allow 118,591 Jewish citizens to move to Israel or to join their families in other countries. Thanks to President Carter's efforts, the government of Indonesia released thirty thousand political prisoners from jail. His attention to human rights made a huge difference throughout the world. Jimmy used the power of the United States to bring about changes in the way governments treated their citizens.

Many of Jimmy's new programs expanded human rights at home too. He created a Department of Education and passed laws to improve the schools, provide loans for college students, and create job-training programs. As president, Jimmy Carter expanded the role of women and African-Americans in government. When he left office, there were forty-six women serving as federal judges. He had appointed forty-one of them. Three out of the fourteen members of his cabinet were women: the secretary of commerce, Juanita Kreps; the secretary of health and human services, Patricia Harris; and the secretary of education, Shirley Hufstedler. Jimmy appointed sixteen women as ambassadors to other countries, and Andrew Young, an African-American from Georgia, became ambassador to the United Nations. Jimmy felt that appointing talented women and people of color to important jobs showed other nations that the United States had changed. Vice President Mondale later said that Jimmy Carter worked so hard on human rights because he "believed that every child is a child of God." Jimmy's faith served as his guide, no matter how difficult the problem.

Chapter 12

Taking Care of God's World

Jimmy worried about the nation's energy problems. Beginning a few years before Jimmy took office, Americans faced shortages of gas and oil. Not only did prices increase, but many gas stations closed because they had no gas to sell. Heating oil was in short supply too. These problems put energy at the top of the list of issues Jimmy intended to tackle.

Two weeks after taking office, he held a fireside chat with the American people. Dressed in a warm sweater, he sat beside a cozy fireplace at the White House and asked people to turn down the heat. He said, "All of us must learn to waste less energy. If we learn to live **thriftily** and learn the importance of helping our neighbors, then we can find ways to adjust." If every family used less energy, energy use nationwide would drop. As use dropped, so would prices. Jimmy tried to convince people that using less energy today saves energy for the future. He asked people to lower their heat to sixty-five degrees during the day and to fifty-five degrees at night.

Jimmy led by example. He lowered the temperature in the White House. It got so chilly that Rosalynn wore long underwear all day long. During the summer, he turned off the air conditioning, and the temperature inside the White House soared to one hundred degrees. When he learned that there were 325 televisions and 220 radios in the White House, Jimmy ordered dozens of them unplugged. He did not expect the American people to do something he wasn't willing to do himself.

President Carter developed an energy plan. He wanted the United States to reduce its use of foreign oil and to find other sources of energy. Members of Congress discussed and debated Jimmy's energy proposals for months. It took three years before they passed the bill. It encouraged companies to build cars that used less gas, home appliances that required less electricity, and houses with better insulation. The energy bill encouraged carpooling, too, and rewarded people for using solar energy in their homes and office buildings. New taxes encouraged people to save energy, and the law required oil companies to set reasonable prices.

It seemed as if almost nothing happened as easily or quickly as President Carter would have liked. Later he remembered the loneliness that he felt as he made important decisions. He wrote, "I prayed a lot—more than ever before in my life—asking God to give me a clear mind, sound judgment, and wisdom in dealing with affairs that could affect the lives of so many people in our own country and around the world."

During his first four months in office, people felt that President Carter was off to a good start. A poll showed that 75 percent of the American people approved of his work. They were pleased that he was dealing with the nation's energy problems. They considered him honest and hardworking.

Worship

The Carters joined First Baptist Church in Washington, DC. In earlier years, Presidents Martin van Buren, Franklin Pierce, Lyndon Johnson, and Harry Truman had worshipped there. The Carters attended worship services at First Baptist Church seventy-three times while Jimmy was president. Amy attended Sunday school and became a baptized member of the church. The Carters always sat in the same pew every week. Before they arrived, the Secret Service checked the area. At the end of the service, the pastor asked the congregation to remain seated until the First Family left. That way, the Carters would not be mobbed by curious well-wishers. The church had followed this same practice years earlier when President Truman had worshipped there.

Wherever the Carters went, crowds followed. That made attending church difficult, but it didn't stop them from going. Many tourists visited First Baptist Church when the Carters attended, and protestors often marched outside.

On fourteen Sundays during his presidency, President Carter taught the church's adult class. About fifty people attended the class, which was held in a large area at the rear balcony of the sanctuary. Rosalynn usually read the scripture and then Jimmy gave the lesson, which was always based on a Bible passage. The members of the class never knew ahead of time whether or not President Carter would be teaching. They enjoyed their regular teacher, but it was a special treat to have the president give the lesson.

Sometimes the Carters went home to Plains for the weekend. Once, unannounced, they went to church in Calhoun, Georgia. Jimmy thanked the congregation for letting him attend, saying, "The fact I was elected president doesn't make me any better than you are, or closer to God."

The Carters spent many Sundays at Camp David in the hills of Maryland. The Carters loved it there and visited sixty-seven times in the four years that Jimmy was president. It was the one place they could worship in privacy. A chaplain from the nearby army base led the service.

Many years after he left Washington, Jimmy revealed a big secret. Sometimes he only pretended to stay at Camp David. Instead, he and Rosalynn went fishing in Pennsylvania. They didn't want reporters tagging along on the fishing trip, so the Carters

Camp David is a country retreat where the president and his family can find peace in the midst of their busy lives. It is located about sixty miles northwest of Washington, DC, in the mountains of Maryland. There are several guest cabins, a pool, tennis courts, biking and hiking trails, and a bowling alley. There's a helicopter pad, too, so presidents and their guests often take a helicopter from the White House directly to Camp David.

took the helicopter to Camp David as if they were staying there. The reporters covered the president's arrival at Camp David and then they headed for motels in a nearby town. That's when Jimmy and Rosalynn slipped back into the helicopter and flew to Spruce Creek in Pennsylvania to fish. Jimmy had loved fishing as a boy. As an adult, he found it fun and relaxing. Jimmy Carter wasn't the only president who enjoyed fishing. George Washington, Chester Arthur, Calvin Coolidge, Herbert Hoover, Dwight Eisenhower, and Grover Cleveland had also shared his love of the sport.

Solving the Panama problem

When he became president, Jimmy had little experience dealing with other countries and world leaders. But he was a man of great energy and determination. He studied the issues, devised plans, and tackled problems that had been developing for years.

One of the first big problems facing President Carter was ownership of the Panama Canal. The ten-mile-wide Canal Zone cut Panama in half. The United States considered the Canal Zone a US territory, but the government of Panama disagreed. In 1964 a riot broke out in the Canal Zone between Panamanians and United States troops stationed there. The situation grew worse. Something had to be done.

Presidents Johnson, Nixon, and Ford had begun work to return the canal to Panama. President Carter carried it through. The treaty promised that the United

States would give up control of the Canal Zone, and that Panama would take over.

On September 7, 1977, eighteen Latin American leaders came to Washington, DC, to watch President Carter and Panama's leader, Omar Torrijos, sign the treaty. The treaty signaled an important change in relationships between the United States and its neighbors to the south.

> The Panama Canal is a man-made waterway that connects the Atlantic and Pacific Oceans. Before the Panama Canal was built, ships had to travel an extra seven thousand miles around the tip of South America to go from one ocean to the other. In 1903, President Theodore "Teddy" Roosevelt signed a treaty with Panama that allowed the United States to build the canal through Panama. The canal is just over fifty-one miles long, and it took six years to complete. Today, over fourteen thousand ships use the canal every year.

Jimmy had promised that he would always deal fairly with other countries. The Panama treaty was proof. The United States Senate approved the canal treaty in 1978. Twenty-two years later, at noon on December 31, 1999, Panama took control of the canal.

Chapter 13

Keeping the Peace

Middle-East peace talks

Long before he became president, Jimmy Carter had been fascinated by the Middle East. As a boy, he had read Bible stories and studied maps of ancient sites. As governor of Georgia, he had visited Israel and seen the places where Jesus had lived and died. As president, he wanted to give the gift of peace to the Middle East.

The modern nation of Israel was founded in 1948 with the strong support of the United States. Jews from all over the world now had a homeland, which was especially important since six million Jews had recently been killed during the Holocaust and World War II (1939–1945). But as more and more Jews settled in Israel, conflicts developed with the Arab Palestinians who lived in the region. Between 1947 and 1973, Israel

President Jimmy Carter (center) worked with Anwar Sadat (left) and Prime Minister Menachem Begin (right) to establish peace in the Middle East.

and its Arab neighbors went to war four times. These wars caused hate and distrust.

Jimmy Carter admired the courage and determination of the Jewish people. He understood their need for a safe homeland. He had never met any Arab leaders until Egypt's president, Anwar Sadat, came to Washington in 1977. The two men talked together about their families, their early lives, and their hometowns. They became friends. By the end of the visit, Jimmy began to hope that peace between Israel and Egypt was possible.

One beautiful summer day, as the Carters walked through the woods at Camp David, Jimmy came up with an idea. Why not invite President Sadat and Israel's prime minister, Menachem Begin, to come to Camp David to talk about peace? How could they fight in such a peaceful place? Rosalynn agreed that it was a good idea. Later though, Jimmy began to have doubts. What if the leaders come and the talks fail? "You've never been afraid of failure before," Rosalynn said.

President Sadat and Prime Minister Begin agreed to join President Carter at Camp David to talk peace. The talks began on September 5, 1978. On the first night, Prime Minister Begin told President Carter that there had not been an agreement between a Jewish nation and Egypt for more than two thousand years. The Carters decided to ask Christians, Muslims, and Jews throughout the world to pray for peace. The plea was sent to the press on the first night of the talks:

> After four wars, despite vast human efforts, the Holy Land does not yet enjoy the blessings of peace. Conscious of the grave issues which face us, we place our trust in the God of our fathers, from whom we seek wisdom and guidance. As we meet here at Camp David, we ask people of all faiths to pray with us that peace and justice may result from these deliberations.

The discussions did not get off to a good start. President Sadat and Prime Minister Begin couldn't agree on anything! After a while, they refused to talk to one another. So Jimmy decided that if they wouldn't talk to each other, they would have to talk through him. He wrote the peace plan, and then he spent the next several days going first to one leader and then to the other to work out the details. It was exhausting work. There were more than fifty issues to discuss, but Jimmy refused to give up.

The secret talks lasted thirteen days. People around the world waited to see if peace was possible. Finally, the leaders reached an agreement called the Camp David Peace Accords. Jimmy Carter earned praise throughout the world for his brilliant leadership.

When President Carter spoke to Congress about the peace accords, both President Sadat and Prime Minister Begin attended. Jimmy turned to them and said, "To these two friends of mine, the words of Jesus—'Blessed are the peacemakers for they shall be the children of God.'" In 1978, Anwar Sadat and Menachem Begin received the Nobel Peace Prize for their efforts to bring peace to the Middle East. They couldn't have done it alone.

Not everyone recognized the important role President Carter had played in reaching a peace agreement, but the members of his Sunday school class did. Someone suggested that the class stand and applaud when he entered the next Sunday. But they decided against it. As one member said, "Politics was not part of the class. We Baptists are strong on separation of Church and State."

Problems at home and abroad

President Carter continued to have success working with world leaders. He met with Deng Xiaoping, the leader of China, and with Leonid Brezhnev, the leader of the Soviet Union. The Soviet Union, which no longer exists, was a powerful nation that included present-day Russia, the Ukraine, and thirteen other Communist states. Carter and Brezhnev agreed to limit the use of nuclear weapons. Fewer nuclear weapons meant that the world was a safer place.

Despite his success overseas, Jimmy was having problems at home. On the Fourth of July 1979, 90 percent of the gas stations in New York City closed down for lack of gasoline. In Pennsylvania, 80 percent closed. People, who were stuck at home over the holiday, grew angry. Why wasn't the president solving their problems? Why was he traveling to other countries when they didn't have enough gas to drive down the street? People worried about gas shortages, unemployment, and rising prices. Many didn't care about what was happening in faraway countries like Japan.

Jimmy knew that what happened in other countries can have a major effect on life in the United States. That is what happened soon after when a revolt took place in Iran. For many years before Jimmy became president, the United States had been supporting the government of Iran. Past presidents believed that Iran was a good influence in the Middle East. But the Shah, Iran's leader, used the secret police to threaten anyone who disagreed with him. The secret police often used violence against the Iranian people. President Carter warned the Shah that eventually the people would revolt, but the Shah did not listen. In the fall of 1979, Iranian students took over the government. An Iranian religious leader, Ayatollah Khomeini, encouraged the rebels. The Shah fled Iran. So did thousands of Americans who lived and worked there. Many of those who stayed worked at the United States Embassy. For a while, the situation improved.

More problems developed when the Shah became ill. He asked if he could visit the United States for medical treatment. US officials in Iran spoke with Iran's new leaders. Would there be trouble if the United States let the Shah come to an American hospital? Iranian officials promised that no harm would come to Americans still living in Iran.

President Carter agreed to let the Shah enter a New York hospital. There were protests and demonstrations in Iran, but President Carter was not too worried. After all, the Iranian officials had said that Americans would be safe.

They were wrong! On November 4, 1979, demonstrators in the Iranian capital of Tehran stormed the United States Embassy. They captured sixty-six Americans. They planned to hold the Americans until the United States returned the Shah to Iran for trial. Jimmy was stunned. It was the worst day of his presidency.

Newspaper and television reports showed pictures of the **hostages**, blindfolded and surrounded by angry crowds. President Carter tried talking to Iranian officials, but they would not let the hostages go. President Carter ordered American banks to freeze all the money in their vaults that belonged to Iran or Iranian businesses. This meant that no one could withdraw the money from the banks. A few days later, thirteen hostages—all women and African-Americans—were released. The Iranians still held fifty-three American men hostage.

Chapter 14

Endings

Many people wanted President Carter to send troops to rescue the hostages and end the crisis, but he was determined to find a peaceful solution. The criticism grew louder. Jimmy tried not to ignore it. His goal was to keep the peace. He later said that it was his mother who gave him the strength to deal with all the criticism. She taught him to be independent. What mattered was doing the right thing. Jimmy was convinced that keeping the peace was the right thing to do, even though many people did not agree.

Jimmy never forgot the hostages. They were on his mind every single day. People all over America prayed for their release. Penne Laingen, the wife of one of the hostages, came up with a way for people to honor them. She suggested that everyone tie yellow ribbons around the trees in their yards. The song "Tie A Yellow Ribbon

Round the Ole Oak Tree" had been a big hit a few years earlier. People all over the country remembered the song. They adopted Penne's idea. Yellow ribbons flew all across the United States until the hostages were released. There was even a yellow ribbon on a tree in the White House yard. Rosalynn Carter placed it there.

A second term?

Jimmy's four-year term as president was coming to an end. He still had lots of work to do. In addition to releasing the hostages, he wanted to improve the schools, hospitals, and prisons. He wanted to continue his work on human rights, as well as to create more jobs and control rising prices. He needed another four-year term to get everything done. In December 1979, Jimmy Carter announced he would run for a second term as president. His family had already started campaigning. They were good at it.

Jimmy stayed close to the White House. He was doing everything possible to get the hostages released— everything except sending troops to Iran. He tried reasoning with Iran, but reason wasn't working. Meanwhile, months of planning had gone into a top-secret rescue mission called Operation Eagle Claw. Jimmy had hoped he wouldn't have to use it, but he finally agreed. Eight helicopters flew a highly trained military rescue team to a secret desert location to begin the rescue—without success.

Jimmy waited by the telephone for news on the rescue. It was one of the worst days of his life. The news was terrible. Not only did the mission fail, but eight men died when a wind storm caused one of the helicopters to crash. Jimmy later wrote, "Some of the loneliest and most difficult decisions in government involve the use of military force. The president, as commander in chief, can cause or prevent the massive loss of human life." The memory of Operation Eagle Claw haunted him for years.

Jimmy continued to look for other ways to bring the hostages home. He still had the Iranian money locked up in banks, and he hoped to use it to bargain for the hostages. Secret talks continued, but Jimmy did not dare make any promises that the hostages would be freed soon. If he failed, people would lose faith in him and he would lose his chance at a second term.

Saying good-bye

At the Democratic National Convention, the delegates selected Jimmy Carter as their candidate for another term as president. He would be running against Ronald Reagan, the Republican candidate. When the two candidates debated one another, over a hundred million people watched on television. It was the largest audience ever to watch a presidential debate. Jimmy Carter gave honest, thoughtful answers, but Ronald Reagan appeared more relaxed and confident. The majority of voters decided that Ronald Reagan was the man to solve their problems. In the 1980 election, the voters elected Ronald Reagan their next president.

The loss hit the Carters hard. Amy would have to leave the friends and school she loved in Washington.

Rosalynn felt bitter. She knew how hard Jimmy had worked, and she knew how much he cared about the American people. How could they reject him? Jimmy feared that the progress he had made to protect human rights and the environment would stop under the new president.

But losing the election didn't mean quitting. President Carter worked just as hard his last months in office as he had before—maybe even harder. He convinced Congress to pass several new laws. One was the Alaska Land Bill. It protected 104.3 million acres of land in Alaska. The Alaska Land Bill more than doubled the size of America's national parks. President Carter called it the "conservation decision of the century."

During their last weeks in the White House, the Carters were overwhelmed with visitors. Friends and family flocked to the White House to spend one more night in the mansion. Amy bid farewell to her school friends. Rosalynn attended farewell parties, packed everyone's belongings, and took pictures of the rooms that they had called home for four years.

On January 4, 1981, President Carter taught Sunday school at First Baptist Church in Washington for the final time. He based his last lesson on words from Luke 9:46–48:

An argument started among the disciples as to which of them would be the greatest. Jesus, knowing their thoughts, took a little child and had him stand beside him. Then he said to them, "Whoever welcomes this little child in my name welcomes me; and whoever welcomes me welcomes the one who sent me. For it is the one who is least among you all who is the greatest.

Jimmy asked if "greatness" comes from being president or a world leader. No, he said, answering his own question. Greatness comes from serving others. As the lesson ended, he said, "If you act like Jesus, you'll be good Christians." Even though he was leaving the office of president, Jimmy Carter planned to keep right on serving others.

Jimmy spent the very last day of his presidency negotiating for the release of the hostages. He later wrote:

The hostages sometimes seemed like part of my own family. I knew them by name, was familiar with their careers, had read their personal letters written from within their prisons in Iran. I knew and had grown to love some of the members of their families... More than anything else, I wanted those American prisoners to be free.

Jimmy didn't sleep at all his last night in the White House. He sat by the phone waiting for word from Iran. An agreement was close. Would it happen in time? If the Iranians did not make a deal before Jimmy left office, the process would have to begin all over again when the next president took office.

At long last, the news arrived. Iran agreed to release the hostages. However, the government of Iran waited until Ronald Reagan took the oath of office to let the hostages go. It was a final insult to Jimmy Carter, but all that really mattered to him was that the hostages were free. The Carters were flying home to Georgia when they learned that the hostages were safe in American hands. Jimmy grasped Rosalynn's hand and together they thanked God.

Chapter 15

Going Home

Rain poured down on the Carters when they reached Plains. Even so, more than three thousand neighbors, friends, and supporters gathered to welcome them home with a potluck supper. They called it, "The world's largest covered-dish dinner." A band played, and friends cheered as Jimmy and Rosalynn danced a waltz. Then Jimmy and Rosalynn walked to their house. A few hours later, Jimmy boarded a plane for Germany where he greeted the newly released hostages. When he finally returned to Plains, he slept for nearly twenty-four hours.

After months of exhausting work and campaigning, Jimmy and Rosalynn needed a vacation. They went to a national park in the Virgin Islands for ten days. They spent time reading and sleeping, and when their energy returned, they went swimming, fishing, sailing, and hiking. They even learned to windsurf. But the Carters did not intend to spend the rest of their lives on vacation. They had work to do.

They unpacked and got Amy settled in school. Jimmy and Rosalynn found life in Plains relaxing and enjoyable after the busy years in politics. President Carter set up a woodworking shop in his garage. The equipment was a gift from his Washington staff, and it was perfect. Once everything was set up, he climbed into a limousine surrounded by Secret Service agents and set off for a lumber store to buy wood. His first project was to install a new wooden floor in the attic. He took up woodworking with the same enthusiasm he poured into other favorite activities like fishing and hunting.

Rosalynn began baking bread. Together, Jimmy and Rosalynn planted a garden. Homegrown vegetables overflowed the kitchen shelves. So did the wild plums, blackberries, and persimmons that Jimmy and Rosalynn gathered during their walks in the nearby woods. They became experts at canning, freezing, and preserving vegetables and fruits. Not only did they taste delicious, but they were healthy too. The Carters hiked and biked through the countryside. They've always valued exercise and a healthy diet.

The Carters were surrounded by friends and family. They even had important overseas visitors. Egyptian President Anwar Sadat and his wife visited the Carters in Plains. Rosalynn made them lunch, and Jimmy introduced the Egyptian leaders to his friends and neighbors. President Sadat even joined the Carters at church.

Soon after Sadat left, Jimmy and Rosalynn traveled to China and Japan. Chinese newspapers printed front-page pictures of Jimmy jogging along China's Great Wall. Chinese leaders honored Jimmy as a peacemaker, as did the people of Japan.

No sooner had Jimmy and Rosalynn returned to Plains than Israel's Prime Minister Begin arrived for a friendly visit. So did the former president of France, Giscard d'Estaing and several of the men who had been held hostage in Iran. They shared tales of their capture and release. These visits and trips lifted Jimmy's spirits. He was enjoying life in Plains, and he began to think about the future in exciting new ways.

Jimmy and Rosalynn spent time discussing their years in Washington. Jimmy began work on a book called *Keeping Faith* about his years as president. "There is no doubt I could have done some things better," he wrote, but he was proud that his administration had passed an amazing number of new laws and programs. There was the energy program, the Panama Canal Treaty, and the Camp David Accords. His most satisfying accomplishments had to do with human rights and peace. As he now says:

I not only kept my own country at peace, but I was one of the few presidents in history that never dropped a bomb or never launched a missile, never fired a bullet . . . . and we also brought peace to other people.

The first building project

When Jimmy left Washington, all his presidential papers had come with him. They filled twenty-four moving trucks! Jimmy knew that building a permanent home for the presidential papers was his job. But he wasn't excited about the project—at least not until he came up with a new idea. He wanted to create "a place to resolve conflicts," he told Rosalynn, a place that would recreate the atmosphere at Camp David where he had helped create an agreement between Egypt and Israel. "There is no place like that now," he said. He also wanted to provide help to nations like the Sudan and Ethiopia where thousands of people were dying in civil wars or from hunger and disease. So Jimmy brought his energy and enthusiasm to a new project. The Carter Center would be not only a presidential library. It would be a one-of-a-kind peace-making and problem-solving center. The Carter Center became Jimmy Carter's gift to the world.

> The United States has thirteen presidential libraries. They are not like regular libraries. They are more like museums and research centers. They house the papers and records created during a president's time in office, photographs of the president and his family, and gifts the president received from foreign governments. Historians and writers use the libraries for research.

Sunday school

The Carters joined Maranatha Baptist Church, a new church that formed while they were in Washington. Jimmy took his turn mowing the church lawn, and he

Today Jimmy Carter teaches Sunday school in Plains.

offered to teach Sunday school. At first, church members were pleased. Then tourists flooded the church, eager for a glimpse of the former president and first lady. "People were standing up to take pictures. They were talking. It was not worship; it was entertainment," church member Jan Williams said. "We had members going home because there was not room to sit."

Church members realized that they had a special opportunity to share their faith with others, but they had to develop a plan. They set aside a section of seats for church members. They greeted visitors at the door and explained how they expected visitors to behave. For example, they allow visitors to take a few quick photos of President Carter when he greets them, but then they must put the cameras away and sit quietly for the lesson and the worship service that follows.

For the past thirty years, Jimmy Carter has taught Sunday school whenever he is home. He begins by asking, "Do we have any visitors?" The answer is always yes. Over the years, people from every US state and many continents have attended the class. There are always a few Baptists, but people come from many different churches. Some have never been to church before—anywhere.

After Sunday school, President and Mrs. Carter attend the worship service. A Secret Service agent stands quietly nearby. When he returned to Plains, Jimmy Carter lived the words he had spoken during his last Sunday school class in Washington, DC. He intended to serve God by serving others—both at church and in the larger community.

Chapter 16

The Gift of Peace

Habitat for Humanity

One summer day in 1984, Jimmy Carter put on his blue jeans and plaid work shirt, picked up a hammer, and joined a Habitat for Humanity house-building crew in Americus, Georgia. He had met some of the volunteers at church. Their faith and dedication to helping others impressed him. After working with them, he was hooked. He realized that Habitat wasn't a charity; it was a chance for people in need of a home to own one.

A few weeks later, when Jimmy visited New York City to give a speech, he stopped by a Habitat project there. Habitat volunteers were turning an old six-story building on East Sixth Street into twenty new apartments. When Jimmy visited, the project was just a big pile of rubble. "Well," he said. "I can see you've got some work ahead of you here."

The Carters work on at least one Habitat for Humanity project every year since 1986.

"Why don't you come back with a group from your church for a work week?" the project leader asked.

Jimmy thought about it and agreed. He recruited friends and neighbors from Georgia and arranged for a bus to take them the 989 miles to New York. Rosalynn and Jimmy rode the bus along with everyone else. They brought their own tools and slept on cots in New York's Metro Baptist Church. No former president or first lady had ever done anything like it.

No Habitat project had ever received so much publicity. Newspaper reporters showed up at the work site, television cameras rolled, and crowds gathered to shout, "Go, Jimmy, go." Money poured into the Habitat office. Local construction companies contributed supplies. Office workers stopped by to drop off a box of nails for the project or a bottle of soda for the workers. Churches collected special offerings for Habitat.

> Habitat for Humanity is a Christian housing project that began in Americus, Georgia in 1976. Volunteers help to build or renovate houses for people in need. The people who receive Habitat homes contribute about five hundred hours of work on their new house, and they repay the cost over time.

As the week ended, Jimmy told a packed audience that Habitat's next project would be to build homes for poor people in the country of Nicaragua. "We want the folks down there to know that some American Christians love them," he said.

Jimmy and Rosalynn were so thrilled by the success of the work project that they began holding an annual Jimmy Carter Work Project. Every year since 1986, Jimmy and Rosalynn have hosted a project either in the United States or overseas.

Today, Jimmy and Rosalynn Carter are Habitat's most famous volunteers. Their willingness to work for Habitat has attracted thousands of other volunteers. Some give money; others bring their hammers. By 2011, Habitat had built over 400,000 houses for more than two million people all over the world.

Teaching and writing

Jimmy also teaches college. Emory University in Atlanta offered him a position as a professor. He's been working there for thirty years. He gives lectures in each of the university's many departments, sharing what he had learned as president. For instance, in history classes he might talk about the American political system. In religion class, he may discuss how faith influences decisions. He gives lectures in English, law, political science, and science classes. Every September he meets with several thousand first-year students. They ask questions, and he gives honest answers. He never runs out of things to say.

Both Jimmy and Rosalynn Carter are authors. By 2011, Jimmy Carter had written twenty books, Rosalynn had written four, and they wrote one book together. The books include autobiographies, histories, religious books, poetry, and even a children's picture book, *The Little Baby Snoogle-Fleejer.* Amy did the artwork. Jimmy Carter is the first and only president to write a novel. *The Hornet's Nest*, published in 2003, is a 480-page novel about the Revolutionary War.

The Carter Center

Jimmy's work as a church leader, teacher, writer, and home-builder has helped thousands of people. But it is his work for the Carter Center that has helped millions. From the beginning, he relied on experts to help design and plan the Carter Center's many programs. The presidential library, which is an important resource for historians, was only a small part of the Carter Center. The Carter Center developed programs to provide food to starving people, medicines to those in pain, and peace to a world often at war.

Jimmy gathered experts in many different areas to help. One of the first programs focused on peace. Beginning in 1983, Jimmy arranged conferences with world leaders to bring peace to troubled areas of the world. Since then he has visited many regions of the world to try to stop the fighting. He has helped resolve conflicts and prevent wars in Haiti, Sudan, Uganda, Liberia, Nepal, Korea, and many other places.

The Carter Center continues President Carter's work on human rights by helping to free political prisoners around the world. Many times Jimmy Carter has written letters urging a leader to release prisoners. Often, Jimmy's words have worked. Other times, he has traveled overseas to personally arrange for a prisoner's freedom. For example, in August 2010, he traveled to North Korea to help Aijalon Gomes, an American who had been teaching English in South Korea. Gomes had visited China, and he made the mistake of crossing over the North Korean border. North Korean soldiers captured him and accused him of spying. Gomes was sentenced to eight years in a North Korean prison camp. Jimmy Carter brought him home seven months after the trial. Gomes is not the only one who owes his freedom to Jimmy Carter. Carter's efforts have freed hundreds of others.

Fair elections

In 1989, President George H. W. Bush asked Jimmy to go to Panama to make sure that Panama's elections were fair and honest. Free elections are often a first step in establishing a government that protects the rights of its citizens. In Panama, Jimmy noticed serious problems. After the voting ended, he gave a speech in Spanish declaring that the elections were dishonest. The people of Panama trusted Jimmy Carter, and soon the government was forced to change.

When trusted, outside observers like Jimmy Carter oversee an election, voters know that they can vote safely and secretly. Since the Panama election, Jimmy has overseen elections in Africa, Latin America, and Asia. By 2011, Carter Center observers had been invited to monitor eighty-three different elections in thirty-four different countries.

Food and medicine

When he was a peanut farmer, Jimmy learned how to make his land more productive. He was convinced that better farming could help farmers in Africa, too, where hunger was killing millions. Through the Carter Center he has helped more than eight million farmers in fifteen African nations to double or triple their harvests. More food means fewer starving people.

When he learned that 3.5 million children were dying because they didn't get vaccinations against common childhood diseases, Jimmy launched a Carter Center program called "Shot of Love." The program began in three countries—Colombia (South America), India (Asia), and Senegal (Africa). It grew to include dozens of other nations and to save millions of lives.

The Carter Center's health programs focus on many neglected diseases. These are diseases that no longer exist in the developed world, but that affect millions of

Louise Gubb/The Carter Center

In 2007, Jimmy and Rosalynn visited Ethiopia to distribute life-saving bed nets in the fight against malaria.

people in Latin America and Africa. Guinea worm disease is one of these neglected diseases. In 1986, about 3.5 million people in Africa and Asia suffered from guinea worm disease. It is caused by drinking water containing guinea worm eggs. They grow inside humans, causing great pain and distress. Carter Center scientists found ways to prevent this disease by filtering the water. In 2010, there were only 1,797 known cases in the world. Soon, the disease may be gone forever.

Today, Jimmy and Rosalynn Carter are working through the Carter Center to prevent two diseases which cause blindness: river blindness and trachoma. They are also fighting many other diseases, like malaria, that kill or disable millions of children throughout the world.

A world leader

Today, Jimmy Carter is one of the world's most respected leaders, even though he doesn't hold any official political office. In 2002, the Nobel Prize Committee awarded Jimmy Carter the Nobel Peace Prize for his "decades of untiring effort to find peaceful solutions to international conflicts, to advance democracy and human rights, and to promote economic and social development." He has received dozens of other honors including the United Nations Human Rights Award, the Presidential Medal of Honor, and the American Peace Award. When he looks back at his many different roles in life, he says, "My life since I left the White House has been most enjoyable and gratifying and unpredictable and adventurous."

He's also received lots of criticism. Jimmy knows that he can't please everyone. He once told his Sunday school class that Christians should "serve God with boldness, and who knows what wonders the Lord may work." When he faces a difficult decision, he asks, "What would Jesus do?" Following the teaching of Christ is more important than the awards or anything else.

Waging peace

On some days, the Carters live a quiet life in Plains. Jimmy still works with wood, and he enjoys painting. Rosalynn spends time enjoying her garden. They shop at the Dollar General store, attend services at Maranatha Church, and go fishing. Other days, they go to Atlanta where Jimmy teaches at Emory University or attends

In 2002, Jimmy Carter received the Nobel Peace Prize for his tireless efforts to find peaceful solutions to world problems.

meetings at the Carter Center. There's a small apartment in the Carter Center with a pull-down bed where they stay overnight.

Family is important to the Carters. They celebrate family events and take vacations with their children, grandchildren, and great-grandchildren. Their oldest grandson, Jason, has followed his grandfather into politics. He's serving in the Georgia State Senate, just like Jimmy did.

Much of the Carters's time is still spent traveling the world for the Carter Center, resolving conflicts, observing elections, freeing political prisoners, and overseeing health programs. Rosalynn calls it "building hope." Jimmy calls it "waging peace."

What Can You Do?

You can be a peacemaker. Jimmy Carter believes that it takes all of us to make the world a more peaceful place. As he says, peace "begins in your family or in your own classroom as you start learning how to deal with the differences that are in everybody's life on a daily basis, and then try to resolve them peacefully."

Whenever a conflict develops, ask yourself:

- What can I do to settle my differences peacefully?
- How can I put into practice the teachings of Jesus Christ?

Jesus teaches us to try to understand people and to forgive them rather than to punish them or hold a grudge. That's not always easy—but it is possible! If you can't find a way to get along with a brother or sister or a classmate on your own, ask for help. Talk to a parent, Sunday school teacher, or an adult you can trust. Peace begins at home. If you learn to be a peacemaker at home, you can carry those skills into the world. As Jesus said in Matthew 5:9: "Blessed are the peacemakers, for they will be called children of God."

You can be a lifesaver by helping the Carter Center to fight malaria. Malaria is a deadly disease caused by the bite of an infected mosquito. Malaria causes high fevers and flu-like symptoms. Every year about 350–500 million people suffer from malaria. It strikes hardest at children five years old and younger. About 90 percent of all cases of malaria are in Africa where one out of every ten children dies of malaria before the age of five.

The Carter Center has found a solution. In Ethiopia and Nigeria, the Carter Center gives free bed nets to families. Sleeping under these nets prevents mosquito bites. The nets are treated with a poison that kills the mosquitoes, too, preventing them from biting others. Each bed net costs six dollars. It's a small price to pay to save a child's life.

Gift of Peace

You can help the Carter Center supply bed nets to children in Africa. Save your allowance, earn money doing chores or errands, or collect donations from family and friends. You can donate on the web or send your donations to:

The Carter Center
One Copenhill
453 Freedom Parkway
Atlanta, GA 30307-1496

Online: Go to the website and click on the button that says, "DONATE NOW."

http://www.cartercenter.org

Glossary

administer to give; to bring into use

campaign a competition between rival politicians running for political office

candidate a person who seeks office

discrimination showing a difference or favoritism based on the group or class, like race, to which a person belongs

economy the management of the income and expenses of a household, business, or country

Great Depression a period during the 1930s when there were worldwide economic problems and mass unemployment

hostage a person held prisoner for political reasons

inauguration a ceremony to place someone in office

integrate to bring together

kerosene a kind of oil used in lamps and heaters

nuclear energy energy created by splitting atoms

nuclear weapon a weapon whose destructive power comes from nuclear energy; atomic bomb

possum informal name for an opposum

primary an election in which voters of each party select candidates for office

revival a church service or series of services designed to renew a community's faith

segregation the practice or policy of creating separate facilities within the same society for the use of a minority group

thriftily clever management of money or resources

Timeline

October 1, 1924	James Earl Carter Jr. is born in Plains, Georgia.
1930	Jimmy Carter enters first grade at Plains Elementary School.
1941	Jimmy Carter graduates from high school; begins classes at Georgia Southwestern College in Americus.
1942	Jimmy Carter transfers to Georgia Institute of Technology in Atlanta.
1943	Jimmy Carter enters the US Naval Academy in Annapolis.
1946	Jimmy Carter receives a naval commission, marries Rosalynn Smith, and moves to Norfolk, Virginia.
1946–1952	Jimmy and Rosalynn Carter move several times to different navy bases; three sons are born: Jack in 1947, Chip in 1950, and Jeff in 1952.
1953	James Earl Carter Sr. dies of cancer; Jimmy Carter moves his family back to Plains where he takes over father's business and becomes involved with the church and the community.
1962–66	Jimmy Carter is elected to Georgia State Senate; serves two terms.
1966	Carter runs for Georgia governor; loses election.
1967	Daughter Amy Carter is born.
1967–1968	Jimmy Carter spends a few weeks doing mission work for Baptist churches in Pennsylvania and Massachusetts.
1971	Jimmy Carter is elected governor of Georgia.

1974	Carter announces his plan to run for president and begins to campaign.
1975	Carter publishes his first book, *Why Not the Best?*
1976	Jimmy Carter wins the presidential election.
January 20, 1977	Carter is inaugurated the 39th president of the United States.

1977 Carter explains energy proposal; signs Panama Canal treaties; reaches weapons agreement with Soviet Union.

1978 Carter meets at Camp David with leaders of Egypt and Israel to develop peace plan [Camp David Accords]; signs National Energy Act. Shah of Iran visits Washington.

1979 Revolt in Iran; Egypt–Israel Peace Treaty signed in March; Carter and Soviet Premier Brezhnev sign SALT II in June; sixty-six Americans taken hostage in Iran on November 4.

1980 Carter runs for a second term in office; Iraq invades Iran in September; Carter debates Republican candidate Ronald Reagan in July; Reagan defeats Carter on November 4.

1981 Carter reaches agreement with Iranians to release American hostages on January 20; Ronald Reagan inaugurated as president; Carter returns to Plains; Egyptian President Sadat and Israeli Prime Minister Begin visit Plains.

1982 Carter Center is founded; Carter begins teaching at Emory University.

1987 Jimmy Carter Presidential Library opens in Atlanta.

1998 Carter receives first United Nations Human Rights Prize.

Gift of Peace

2002 Carter is awarded the Nobel Peace Prize.

2011 By 2011, the Carter Center under Jimmy
Carter's leadership has monitored eighty-three
elections in thirty-four countries, promoted
peace, and fought deadly diseases. He has
taught at Emory University for thirty years,
and is Habitat for Humanity's most famous
volunteer.

To Learn More

Visit these places:

Jimmy Carter Library and Museum
441 Freedom Parkway
Atlanta, Georgia 30307
(404) 865–7100

The Jimmy Carter Presidential Library and Museum opened in January 1987. Once the library was built, the materials were sorted and made ready for researchers. Today, the Jimmy Carter Library and Museum contains 27 million pages of White House papers, 500,000 photographs, and hundreds of hours of video recordings and audio tapes.[1] People come from around the world to visit the library and to study its contents.

Jimmy Carter National Historic Site
300 N. Bond Street
Plains, Georgia 31780
(229) 824–4104

The Jimmy Carter National Historic Site gives visitors the chance to visit Jimmy Carter's boyhood farm, the Plains High School, and the train depot. The Carter Farm has been recreated to look like it did in 1938. You can visit Jimmy's boyhood home, stop by the barn, and explore other farm buildings. At various stops along the way, you can listen to a recording of Jimmy Carter talking about his childhood adventures.

Virtually tour Jimmy Carter's boyhood home:

http://www.jimmycartervirtualtour.info/

---

[1] http://www.jimmycarterlibrary.gov/information/preslib.phtml

Check out these websites

Jimmy Carter "Just for Kids"
http://www.jimmycarter.info/justforkids_1.html

The Youth Space at Carter Library

http://www.jimmycarterlibrary.gov/youthspace/

The White House Biography

http://www.whitehouse.gov/about/presidents/jimmycarter

Major Sources

Ariail, Dan and Cheryl Heckler-Feltz. *The Carpenter's Apprentice: The Spiritual Biography of Jimmy Carter*. Grand Rapids: Zondervan, 1996.

Bourne, Peter G. *Jimmy Carter: A Comprehensive Biography from Plains to Postpresidency*. New York: Scribner, 1997.

Brinkley, Douglas. *The Unfinished Presidency: Jimmy Carter's Journey Beyond the White House*. New York: Viking, 1998.

Carter, Jimmy. *Always a Reckoning, and Other Poems*. New York: Times Books, 1995.

————. *Beyond the White House: Waging Peace, Fighting Disease, Building Hope*. New York: Simon & Schuster, 2007.

————. *An Hour Before Daylight: Memories of a Rural Boyhood*. New York: Simon & Schuster, 2001.

————. *Keeping Faith: Memoirs of a President*. Fayetteville, AR: University of Arkansas Press, 1995.

————. Illustrated by Amy Carter. *The Little Baby Snoogle-Fleejer*. New York: Times Books, 1996.

————. *Living Faith*. New York: Random House, 2001.

————. *An Outdoor Journal*. Fayetteville, AR: University of Arkansas Press, 1994.

————. *A Remarkable Mother*. New York: Simon & Schuster, 2008.

————. *Sharing Good Times*. New York: Simon & Schuster, 2005.

————. *The Spiritual Journey of Jimmy Carter, in His Own Words*, compiled by Wesley G. Pippert. New York: Macmillan, 1978.

————. *Talking Peace: A Vision for the Next Generation*. New York: Dutton, 1993.

————. *Turning Point: A Candidate, a State, and a Nation Come of Age*. New York: Times Books, 1992.

————. *Why Not the Best? Why One Man is Optimistic about America's Third Century*. Nashville: Broadman Press, 1975.

Carter, Jimmy. Telephone interview with author, March 17, 2011.

Carter, Rosalynn. *First Lady from Plains*. Boston: Houghton Mifflin, 1984.

Kaufman, Burton I. *The Presidency of James Earl Carter, Jr.* Lawrence, KS: University Press of Kansas, 1993.

Krukones, Michael G. "The Campaign Promises of Jimmy Carter: Accomplishments and Failures." *Presidential Studies Quarterly* 15, no. 1 (Winter 1985): 136–144.

Lasky, Victor. *Jimmy Carter: The Man & the Myth*. New York: Richard Marek, 1979.

Maddox, Robert L. *Preacher at the White House*. Nashville: Broadman, 1984.

Mazlish, Bruce and Edwin Diamond. *Jimmy Carter: An Interpretive Biography*. New York: Simon & Schuster, 1979.

Morris, Kenneth E. *Jimmy Carter, American Moralist*. Athens, GA: University of Georgia Press, 1996.

Richardson, Don, ed. *Conversations with Carter*. Boulder, CO: Lynne Reinner, 1998.

Zelizer, Julian E. *Jimmy Carter*. The American Presidents series, edited by Arthur M. Schlesinger Jr. and Sean Wilentz. New York: Times Books, 2010.

The Carter Center

"Ultimately, the work of the Carter Center is about helping people achieve better opportunities and watching hope take root where it languished before." —Jimmy Carter

The Carter Center, in partnership with Emory University, is guided by a fundamental commitment to human rights and the alleviation of human suffering; it seeks to prevent and resolve conflicts, enhance freedom and democracy, and improve health. While the program agenda may change, the Carter Center is guided by five principles:

1. The Center emphasizes action and results. Based on careful research and analysis, it is prepared to take timely action on important and pressing issues.
2. The Center does not duplicate the effective efforts of others.
3. The Center addresses difficult problems and recognizes the possibility of failure as an acceptable risk.
4. The Center is nonpartisan and acts as a neutral in dispute resolution activities.
5. The Center believes that people can improve their lives when provided with the necessary skills, knowledge, and access to resources.

The Carter Center collaborates with other organizations, public or private, in carrying out its mission.

Contact Us:
The Carter Center
One Copenhill
453 Freedom Parkway
Atlanta, GA 30307
Phone: (404) 420–5100 or
(800) 550–3560
E-mail: carterweb@emory.edu

We want to hear from you. Please send your comments about this book to us in care of zreview@zondervan.com. Thank you.

ZONDERVAN.com/
AUTHORTRACKER
follow your favorite authors